WHAT TEACHERS NEED TO KNOW ABOUT ASSESSMENT

The Authors

Lawrence M. Rudner (Ph.D., Catholic University; M.B.A., University of Maryland) heads the ERIC Clearinghouse on Assessment and Evaluation and is the Associate Director of the Maryland Assessment Research Center for Education Success in the Department of Measurement, Statistics, and Evaluation at the University of Maryland, College Park. He has authored numerous papers, and books ranging from formula derivations to understanding patron search strategies on the Web. The principal or co-principal investigator on more than 60 funded projects, Dr. Rudner's current research interests include automated essay scoring and measurement decision theory.

William C. Schafer (Ed.D., University of Rochester) is Affiliated Professor (Emeritus), Maryland Assessment Research Center for Education Success, Department of Measurement, Statistics, and Evaluation, University of Maryland, College Park. A member of the Department faculty for 31 years, he taught numerous applied statistics courses. A former editor of *Measurement and Evaluation in Counseling and Development* and is on the editorial boards of that publication and of *Applied Measurement in Education, Educational and Psychological Measurement.* He is co-editor of *Practical Assessment, Research & Evaluation,* the electronic journal sponsored by ERIC that first published several of the papers in this book. From 1997 to 1999 he served as Director of Student Assessment with the Maryland State Department of Education.

About ERIC

Since its inception in 1966, the Educational Resources Information Center (ERIC) has contributed to American education by increasing and facilitating the use of educational research and information to improve practice in learning, teaching, educational decision making, and research, wherever and whenever these activities take place. ERIC is best known for its bibliographic database of more than one million citations. The ERIC Clearinghouse on Assessment and Evaluation (ERIC/AE) seeks to 1) provide balanced information concerning educational assessment, evaluation, and research methodology; 2) provide resources to encourage the responsible use of educational data; and 3) promote the best resources within its scope. The ERIC Web site (http://ericae.net) features an extensive full-text library, the on-line journal Practical Assessment Research and Evaluation, an award-winning pathfinder to help locate assessment resources, offers answers to Frequently Asked Questions (FAQs) about educational assessment, access to a database of test descriptions, and access to the ERIC database.

ERIC™

Educational Resources Information Center

Student Assessment Series

WHAT TEACHERS NEED TO KNOW ABOUT ASSESSMENT

Lawrence M. Rudner
William D. Schafer

Glen W. Cutlip
Series Editor

NATIONAL EDUCATION ASSOCIATION

Note

The National Education Association commissioned this book with the intention of making available to educators a single wide-spectrum work on student assessment, containing both original new selections and edited reprints of important articles collected in the Educational Resources Information Clearinghouse on Assessment and Evaluation (ERIC/AE).

ERIC staff members' time for this project was sponsored in part with funding from the Office of Educational Research and Improvement (OERI), U.S. Department of Education, under contact ED99C00032.

The opinions expressed in this publication should not be construed as representing the policy or position of the National Education Association, nor do they necessarily reflect the positions or policies of OERI or the U.S. Department of Education. These materials are intended to be discussion documents for educators who are concerned with specialized interests of the profession.

Library of Congress Cataloguing-in-Publication data.

Rudner, Lawrence M.
   What teachers need to know about assessment/Lawrence M. Rudner,
   William D. Schafer. p. cm. — (Student assessment series)
   ISBN 0-8106-2074-X
   1. Educational tests and measurements—United States. 2.
Examinations—United States—Design and construction. 3.
Examinations—United States—Scoring. I. Schafer, William D. II. Title.
III. Series.

LB3051 .R815 2002
371.26'2—dc21   2002016607

CONTENTS

Part 3: Essential Skills for Students

INTRODUCTION

Testing and assessment have become a daily concern in American education. Evidence of this is in the test results or testing ideas appearing in the popular press as well as in the actions of the state or district superintendent's office.

Testing is more than accountability and at its best, it can be a means to improve education. Standardized tests and large-scale assessments can and are being used to encourage teaching of the skills prescribed by state and local agencies. A critical component of instruction, various forms of teacher assessment permeate everyday classroom activity. Paper and pencil tests provide a formal indication of what has and has not been learned. Routine questioning and the evaluation of projects and activities in the classroom and other forms of assessment are close to the heart of instruction.

Teachers today, perhaps more than ever before, have a need to be knowledgeable consumers of test information and constructors of assessment instruments and protocols. They even need to teach their students about testing. Few courses and textbooks exist to help meet this need and there are very few materials designed specifically for teachers in the classroom.

The goal of this book is to help educators become knowledgeable users of teacher-constructed and district/state-sponsored assessments. It contains information about:

- fundamental concepts common to all assessments

- essential classroom assessment concepts

- useful concepts and issues pertaining to district, state, and national assessment

This is a very hands-on book, the contents of which can be applied easily. There are checklists, suggestions, guidelines, and very few formulas. The authors take the attitude that any means to gather information about students, whether objective or subjective, is an assessment. Thus, this book talks about teacher-made tests, portfolios, and teacher notes in addition to standardized tests. The book is not intended to replace a semester-long course or two on measurement but, rather, is designed to arm the busy teacher with some tools that will help with everyday survival in today's environment of high-stakes testing and assessment demands

If you like any part of this book, please feel free to photocopy that portion or print it from the free online version and share it with your colleagues. Our goal is to get good, useful information into the hands of teachers.

Part 1: Fundamental Concepts Common to All Assessments addresses the basic concepts of testing and addresses standardized and large-scale assessments—typically the kinds of tests sponsored by state education agencies, reported in the popular press, and, unfortunately, often inappropriately used as the sole measure to judge the worth of a school. Scoring results are discussed, along with the alignment of instruction and testing and the role of testing as a valuable instructional planning tool. The section ends with an overview of the debate over national testing.

Part 2: Essential Concepts for Classroom Assessment. The most frequent and most valuable types of tests are those developed and used by classroom teachers. This section is designed to help the classroom teacher develop and write better multiple choice and performance tests. Special attention is paid to the development of analytic and holistic scoring rubrics. Consistent with the view of testing as a form of data gathering and communication, chapters are included on classroom questioning as part of routine instruction and on written comments on report cards.

Part 3: Essential Skills for Students. The last section is designed to help teachers help their students to understand the concept of testing and to achieve better results on the tests they take. It also contains information that will help students overcome misleading study patterns. The section ends with a chapter actually written for students, emphasizing the need for good study habits and providing a few test-taking tips for different types of exams. The authors hope teachers will feel free to reproduce this final chapter for their own students.

NEA offers this book as a valuable tool for both instruction and assessment.

Glen W. Cutlip
Series Editor

PART I

Fundamental Concepts

Common to All

Assessments

I. ◆

TESTING AND TEACHING

By Lawrence M. Rudner and William D. Schafer

Throughout this book, the term "test" is viewed as any of a variety of techniques that can capture evidence of what a person knows in response to a question. These techniques include standardized and large-scale tests of achievement, teacher-developed paper-and-pencil tests, classroom questions (including interactions that allow teachers to see whether students are ready to move on during instruction), performance tests—any system of collecting data where there is a "correct" response, or responses that are better than others.

In this context, testing and teaching should be intertwined. The information provided by tests in their various forms, should be the tool that guides the instructional process, for both teacher and student. In 1989, Rudman pointed out some instructional roles for educational tests. Those roles haven't changed:

Testing is a Useful Tool at the Beginning of the School Year.

It can help a teacher gain an overview of what students bring to new instruction. Test results early in the school year can help the teacher plan review material and identify potential issues to be faced. Examining past test results can help a teacher who is new to a specific school assess the school setting that he or she will work in, as well as the expectations the school has for his or her students.

Testing Can Aid in Decision-Making about Grouping Students in the Class.

Testing can yield information that will aid the teacher in assigning specific students to instructional groups. The groups can always be changed later after more teaching and testing have taken place.

Testing Can Be Used as a Diagnostic Tool to Indicate What Individual Pupils Know.

No one source of data can be sufficient to yield a full assessment of what a pupil knows about school-related content. What is called for is a corroboration based on several kinds of data drawn from various types of assessment: standardized tests of achievement and aptitude, teacher-made quizzes, observations of behavior, informal interactions, and the like. Diagnosis does not necessarily mean prescription unless the data collected have demonstrated high reliability and validity, that is, you can trust them and they convey what you need to know in order to make instructional decisions about students.

Testing Can Help the Teacher Determine the Pace of Classroom Instruction.

Teachers tend to use tests they have prepared themselves much more often than any other type of test to monitor what students have learned. Teacher-made tests may take the form of oral questioning of the class or individual students, or paper-and-pencil quizzes. Systematic observations of a student applying a skill can be thought of as a form of performance testing. Such test techniques, which are prerequisites for determining how quickly new material can be presented, help the teacher gain a perspective of the range of attained learning as well as individual competence.

Tests Can Be Used to Help Make Promotion and Retention Decisions.

Many factors enter into the important decision of moving a student into the next grade. Intuition is an important part of any decision, but that intuition is enhanced when coupled with data. Standardized tests, and records of classroom performance on less formal tests, are essential for supplying much of the data upon which promotion and retention decisions are based.

Test Results are Important Communication Devices for Sharing Information with Boards of Education, Parents, and the General Public Through the Media.

Classroom instruction depends upon a large support network that needs accurate information if an adequate support level is to be maintained. Tests in various forms can supply that information. Informational needs vary among the support groups; specialized referrals for remediation and enrichment need test data for parental support and approval; effectiveness of educational planning is needed by boards of education—evidence which can be partially supplied by test data; financial support of existing programs by the general community requires evidence that can be supplied by test data.

Test Results are Useful Tools for Measuring the Effectiveness of Instruction and Learning.

Various types of tests can be employed when measuring how effectively teaching impacts student learning. Learning can be viewed within a school district at three levels: district, building, and classroom. Standardized tests are particularly useful at all three levels. These tests can be used in norm-, criterion-, and objective-referenced modes. Tests written within the district for large-scale use can also supply information focused specifically on unique local aspects of educational programs.

II.

FUNDAMENTAL ASSESSMENT PRINCIPLES FOR TEACHERS AND SCHOOL ADMINISTRATORS

By James H. McMillan

While several authors have argued that there are a number of "essential" assessment concepts, principles, techniques, and procedures that teachers and administrators need to know about (e.g., Calfee and Masuda,1997; Cizek, 1997; Ebel, 1962; Farr and Griffin, 1973; Fleming and Chambers, 1983; Gullickson, 1985, 1986; Mayo, 1967; McMillan, 2001; Sanders and Vogel, 1993; Schafer, 1991; Stiggins and Conklin, 1992), there continues to be relatively little emphasis on assessment in the preparation of, or professional development of, teachers and administrators (Stiggins, 2000). In addition to the admonitions of many authors, there are established professional standards for assessment skills of teachers, for example *Standards for Teacher Competence in Educational Assessment of Students* (1990), a framework of assessment tasks for administrators (Impara and Plake, 1996), the *Code of Professional Responsibilities in Educational Measurement* (1995), the *Code of Fair Testing Practices* (1988), and the new edition of *Standards for Educational and Psychological Testing* (1999). If that isn't enough information, a project directed by Arlen Gullickson at the Evaluation Center of Western Michigan University will publish in the near future standards for evaluations of students.

The purpose of this chapter is to use suggestions and guidelines from these sources, in light of current assessment demands and contemporary theories of learning and motivation, to present eleven basic principles to guide the assessment training and professional development of teachers and administrators. That is, what is it about assessment, whether large-scale or classroom, that is fundamental for effective understanding and application? What are the "big ideas" that, when well understood and applied, will effectively guide good assessment practices, regardless of the grade level, subject matter, developer, or user of the results? As Jerome Bruner stated many years ago in his classic, *The Process of Education:* "The curriculum of a subject should be determined by the most fundamental understanding that can be achieved of the underlying principles that give structure to that subject." (Bruner, 1960, p. 31). What principles, in other words, provide the most essential, fundamental "structure" of assessment knowledge and skills that result in effective educational practices and improved student learning?

Assessment Is Inherently a Process of Professional Judgment.

The first principle is that professional judgment is the foundation for assessment and, as such, is needed to properly understand and use all aspects of assessment. The measurement of student performance may seem "objective" with such practices as machine scoring and multiple-choice test items, but even these approaches are based on professional assumptions and values. Whether that judgment occurs in constructing test questions, scoring essays, creating rubrics, grading participation, combining scores, or interpreting standardized test scores, the essence of the process is making professional interpretations and decisions. Understanding this principle helps teachers and administrators realize the importance of their own judgments and those of others in evaluating the quality of assessment and the meaning of the results.

Assessment Is Based on Separate but Related Principles of Measurement Evidence and Evaluation.

It is important to understand the difference between measurement evidence (differentiating degrees of a trait by description or by assigning scores) and evaluation (interpretation of the description or scores). Essential measurement-evidence skills include the ability to understand and interpret the meaning of descriptive statistical procedures, including variability, correlation, percentiles, standard scores, growth-scale scores, norming, and principles of combining scores for grading. A conceptual understanding of these techniques (though not necessarily knowing how to compute statistics) is needed for such tasks as interpreting student strengths and weaknesses, as well as reliability and validity evidence, and making grade determination and admissions decisions. Schafer (1991) has indicated that these concepts and techniques comprise part of an essential language for educators. They also provide a common basis for communication about "results," interpretation of evidence, and appropriate use of data. This is increasingly important given the pervasiveness of standards-based, high-stakes, large-scale assessments. Evaluation concerns merit and worth of the data as applied to a specific use or context. It involves what Shepard (2000) has described as the systematic analysis of evidence. Like students, teachers and administrators need analysis skills to effectively interpret evidence and make value judgments about the meaning of the results.

Assessment Decision-Making is Influenced by a Series of Tensions.

Competing purposes, uses, and pressures result in tension for teachers and administrators as they make assessment-related decisions. For example, good teaching is characterized by assessments that motivate and engage students in ways that are consistent with teachers' philosophies of teaching and learning and with theories of development, learning, and motivation. Most teachers want to use constructed-response assessments because they believe this kind of testing is best to ascertain student understanding. On the other hand, factors external to the classroom, such as mandated large-scale testing, promote different assessment strategies, such as using selected-response tests and providing practice in objective test-taking (McMillan and Nash, 2000). Further examples of tensions include the following:

- Learning vs. auditing

- Formative (informal and ongoing) vs. summative (formal and conclusive)

- Criterion-referenced vs. norm-referenced

- Value-added vs. absolute standards

- Traditional vs. alternative

- Authentic vs. contrived

- Speeded tests vs. power tests

- Standardized tests vs. classroom tests

These tensions suggest that decisions about assessment are best made with a full understanding of how different factors influence the nature of the assessment. Once all the alternatives are understood, priorities need to be set; hence trade-offs are inevitable. With an appreciation of the tensions teachers and administrators will hopefully make more informed, better justified assessment decisions.

Assessment Influences Student Motivation and Learning.

Grant Wiggins (1998) has used the term educative assessment to describe techniques and issues that educators should consider when they design and use assessments. His message is that the nature of assessment influences what is learned and the degree of meaningful engagement by students in the learning process. While Wiggins contends that assessments should be authentic, with feedback and opportunities for revision to improve rather than simply audit learning, the more general principle is understanding how different assessments affect students. Will students be more engaged if assessment tasks are problem-based? How do students study when they know the test consists of multiple-choice items? What is the nature of feedback, and when is it given to students? How does assessment affect student effort? Answers to such questions help teachers and administrators understand that assessment has powerful effects on motivation and learning. For example, recent research summarized by Black and Wiliam (1998) shows that student self-assessment skills, learned and applied as part of formative assessment, enhance student achievement.

Assessment Contains Error.

Teachers and administrators need not only to know that there is error in all classroom and standardized assessments, but also more specifically how reliability is determined and how much error is likely. With so much emphasis today on high-stakes testing for promotion, graduation, teacher and administrator accountability, and school accreditation, it is critical that all educators understand concepts such as standard error of measurement, reliability coefficients, confidence intervals, and standard setting. Two reliability principles deserve special attention. The first is that reliability refers to scores, not instruments. Second, teachers and administrators need to understand that, typically, error is underestimated. A recent paper by Rogosa (1999) effectively illustrates the concept of underestimation of error by showing in terms of percentile rank probable true score hit-rate and test-retest results.

Good Assessment Enhances Instruction.

Just as assessment impacts student learning and motivation, it also influences the nature of instruction in the classroom. There has been considerable recent literature promoting assessment as something that is integrated with instruction, and not an activity that merely audits learning (Shepard, 2000). When assessment is integrated with instruction it informs teachers about what activities and assignments will be most useful, what level of teaching is most appropriate, and how summative assessments provide diagnostic information. For instance, during instruction activities informal, formative assessment helps teachers know when to move on, when to ask more questions, when to give more examples, and what responses to student questions are most appropriate. Standardized test scores, when used appropriately, help teachers understand student strengths and weaknesses to target further instruction.

Good Assessment Is Valid.

Validity is a concept that needs to be fully understood. Like reliability, there are technical terms and issues associated with validity that are essential in helping teachers and administrators make reasonable and appropriate inferences from assessment results (e.g., types of validity evidence, validity generalization, construct underrepresentation, construct-irrelevant variance, and discriminant and convergent evidence). Of critical importance is the concept of evidence based on consequences, a new major validity category in the recently revised *Standards for Educational and Psychological Testing*. Both intended and unintended consequences of assessment need to be examined with appropriate evidence that supports particular arguments or points of view. Of equal importance is getting teachers and administrators to understand their roles in gathering and interpreting validity evidence.

Good Assessment Is Fair and Ethical.

Arguably, the most important change in the recently published *Standards for Educational and Psychological Testing* is an entire new major section entitled

"Fairness in Testing." The *Standards* presents four views of fairness: as absence of bias (e.g., offensiveness and unfair penalization), as equitable treatment, as equality in outcomes, and as opportunity to learn. It includes entire chapters on the rights and responsibilities of test takers, testing individuals of diverse linguistic backgrounds, and testing individuals with disabilities or special needs. Three additional areas are also important:

- Student knowledge of learning targets and the nature of the assessments prior to instruction (e.g., knowing what will be tested, how it will be graded, scoring criteria, anchors, exemplars, and examples of performance)

- Student prerequisite knowledge and skills, including test-taking skills

- Avoiding stereotypes.

Good Assessments Use Multiple Methods.

Assessment that is fair, leading to valid inferences with a minimum of error, is a series of measures that show student understanding through multiple methods. A complete picture of what students understand and can do is put together in pieces comprised of different approaches to assessment. While testing experts and testing companies stress that important decisions should not be made on the basis of a single test score, some educators at the local level and some policymakers at the state and national levels seem determined to violate this principle. There is a need to understand the entire range of assessment techniques and methods, with the realization that each has limitations.

Good Assessment Is Efficient and Feasible.

Teachers and school administrators have limited time and resources. Consideration must be given to the efficiency of different approaches to assessment, balancing needs to implement methods required to provide a full understanding with the time needed to develop and implement the methods, and score results. Teacher skills and knowledge are important to consider, as well as the level of support and resources.

Good Assessment Appropriately Incorporates Technology.

As technology advances and teachers become more proficient in the use of technology, there will be increased opportunities for teachers and administrators to use computer-based techniques (e.g., item banks, electronic grading, computer-adapted testing, computer-based simulations), Internet resources, and more complex, detailed ways of reporting results. There is, however, a danger that technology will contribute to the mindless use of new resources, such as using items on-line developed by some companies without adequate evidence of reliability, validity, and fairness, and crunching numbers with software programs without sufficient thought about weighting, error, and averaging.

Summary

To summarize, what is most essential about assessment is understanding how general, fundamental assessment principles and ideas can be used to enhance student learning and teacher effectiveness. This will be achieved as teachers and administrators learn about conceptual and technical assessment concepts, methods, and procedures, for both large-scale and classroom assessments, and apply these fundamentals to instruction.

Note: Earlier versions of this paper were presented at the Annual Meeting of the American Educational Research Association, New Orleans, April 24, 2000 and published as McMillan, James H. (2000). Fundamental Assessment Principles for Teachers and School Administrators. *Practical Assessment, Research & Evaluation, 7(8).* Available online: http://ericae.net/pare/getvn.asp?v=7&n=8.

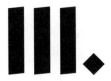

III.

TRADITIONAL AND MODERN CONCEPTS OF VALIDITY

By Amy C. Brualdi

Test validity refers to the degree to which the *inferences* based on test scores are meaningful, useful, and appropriate. Thus test validity is a characteristic of a test when it is administered to a particular population. Validating a test refers to accumulating empirical data and logical arguments to show that the inferences are indeed appropriate.

This chapter introduces the modern concepts of validity advanced by the late Samuel Messick (1989, 1996a, 1996b). We start with a brief review of the traditional methods of gathering validity evidence.

Traditional Concept of Validity

Traditionally, the various means of accumulating validity evidence have been grouped into three categories—content-related, criterion-related, and construct-related. These broad categories are a convenient way to organize and discuss validity evidence. There are no rigorous distinctions between them; they are not distinct types of validity. Evidence normally identified with the criterion-related or content-related categories, for example, may also be relevant in the construct-related category.

Criterion-related validity evidence seeks to demonstrate that test scores are systematically related to one or more outcome criteria. In terms of an achievement test, for example, criterion-related validity may refer to the extent to which a test can be used to draw inferences regarding achievement. Empirical evidence in support of criterion-related validity may include a comparison of performance on the test against performance on outside criteria such as grades, class rank, other tests, and teacher ratings.

Content-related validity evidence refers to the extent to which the test questions represent the skills in the specified subject area. Content validity is often evaluated by examining the plan and procedures used in test construction. Did the test development procedure follow a rational approach that ensures appropriate content? Did the process ensure that the collection of items would represent appropriate skills?

Construct-related validity evidence refers to the extent to which the test measures the "right" psychological constructs. Intelligence, self-esteem, and creativity are examples of such psychological traits. Evidence in support of construct-related validity can take many forms. One approach is to demonstrate that the items within a measure are inter-related and therefore measure a single construct. Inter-item correlation and factor analysis are often used to demonstrate relationships among the items. Another approach is to demonstrate that the test behaves as one would expect a measure of the construct to behave. For example, one might expect a measure of creativity to show a greater correlation with a measure of artistic ability than with a measure of scholastic achievement.

Modern Concept of Validity

Messick (1989, 1996a) argues that the traditional conception of validity is fragmented and incomplete especially because it fails to take into account both evidence of the value implications of score meaning as a basis for action and the social consequences of score use. His modern approach views validity as a unified concept which places a heavier emphasis on how a test is used. Six distinguishable aspects of validity are highlighted as a means of addressing central issues implicit in the notion of validity as a unified concept. In effect, these six aspects conjointly function as general validity criteria or standards for all educational and psychological measurement. These six aspects must be viewed as interdependent and complementary forms of validity evidence and not as separate and substitutable validity types

Content. A key issue for the content aspect of validity is determining the knowledge, skills, and other attributes to be revealed by the assessment tasks. Content standards themselves should be relevant and representative of the construct domain. Increasing achievement levels or performance standards should reflect increases in complexity of the construct under scrutiny and not increasing sources of construct-irrelevant difficulty (Messick, 1996a).

Substansive. The substansive aspect of validity emphasizes the verification of the domain processes to be revealed in assessment tasks. These can be identified through the use of substansive theories and process modeling (Embretson, 1983; Messick 1989). When determining the substansiveness of a test, one should consider two points. First, the assessment tasks must have the ability to provide an appropriate sampling of domain processes in addition to traditional coverage of domain content. Also, the engagement of these samples in these assessment tasks must be confirmed by the accumulation of empirical evidence.

Structure. Scoring models should be rationally consistent with what is known about the structural relations inherent in behavioral manifestations of the construct in question (Loevinger, 1957). The manner in which the execution of tasks is assessed and scored should be based on how the implicit processes of the respondent's actions combine dynamically to produce effects. Thus, the internal structure of the assessment should be consistent with what is known about the internal structure of the construct domain (Messick, 1989).

Generalizability. Assessments should provide representative coverage of the content and processes of the construct domain. This allows score interpretations to be broadly generalizable within the specified construct. Evidence of such generalizability depends on the task's degree of correlation with other tasks that also represent the construct or aspects of the construct.

External Factors. External aspects of validity refers to the extent that the assessment score's relationship with other measures and nonassessment behaviors reflects the expected high, low, and interactive relations implicit in the specified construct. Thus, the score interpretation is substantiated externally by appraising the degree to which empirical relationships are consistent with that meaning.

Consequential Aspects of Validity. It is important to accrue evidence of such positive consequences as well as evidence that adverse consequences are minimal. The consequential aspect of validity includes evidence and rationales for evaluating the intended and unintended consequences of score interpretation and use. This type of investigation is especially important when it concerns adverse consequences for individuals and groups that are associated with bias in scoring and interpretation.

These six aspects of validity apply to all educational and psychological measurement; most score-based interpretations and action inferences either invoke these properties or assume them, explicitly or tacitly. The challenge in test validation, then, is to link these inferences to convergent evidence that supports them as well as to discriminant evidence that discounts plausible rival inferences.

Sources of Invalidity

Two major threats to test validity are worth noting, especially with today's emphasis on high-stakes performance tests.

Construct underrepresentation indicates that the tasks that are measured in the assessment fail to include important dimensions or facets of the construct. Therefore, the test results are unlikely to reveal a student's true abilities within the construct that the test is indicated to measure.

Construct-irrelevant variance means that the test measures too many variables, many of which are irrelevant to the interpreted construct. This type of invalidity can take two forms, construct-irrelevant easiness and construct-irrelevant difficulty. *Construct-irrelevant easiness* occurs when extraneous clues in item or task formats permit some individuals to respond correctly or appropriately in ways that are irrelevant to the construct being assessed; *construct-irrelevant difficulty* occurs when extraneous aspects of the task make it irrelevantly difficult for some individuals or groups. While the first type of construct-irrelevant variance causes a student's score to be higher than it would be under normal circumstances, the latter causes a notably lower score.

Because there is a relative dependence of task responses on the processes, strategies, and knowledge implicated in task performance, one should be able to identify through cognitive-process analysis the theoretical mechanisms underlying task performance (Embretson, 1983).

IV.

Reliability

By Lawrence W. Rudner and William D. Schafer

All tests contain error. This is true of both tests in the physical sciences and psychological tests. In measuring length with a ruler, for example, there may be systematic error associated with where the zero point is printed on the ruler and random error associated with the eye's ability to read the marking and extrapolate between the markings. It is also possible that the length of the object can vary over time and environment (e.g., with changes in temperature). One goal in assessment is to keep such errors down to levels appropriate for the purposes of a given test. High-stakes tests, such as licensure examinations, should have very little error. Classroom tests can tolerate more error as it is fairly easy to spot and correct mistakes made during the testing process. Reliability focuses only on the degree of errors that are nonsystematic, called *random errors.*

Reliability has been defined in different ways by different authors. Perhaps the best way to define reliability is the extent to which the measurements from a test are the result of characteristics of those being measured. For example, reliability has elsewhere been defined as "the degree to which test scores for a group of test takers are consistent over repeated applications of a measurement procedure and hence are inferred to be dependable and repeatable for an individual test taker" (Berkowitz, Wolkowitz, Fitch, and Kopriva, 2000). This definition will be satisfied if the scores are indicative of properties of the test takers; otherwise they will vary unsystematically and not be repeatable or dependable.

Reliability can also be viewed as an indicator of the absence of random error when the test is administered. When random error is minimal, scores can be expected to be more consistent from administration to administration.

Technically, the theoretical definition of reliability is the proportion of score variance caused by systematic variation in the population of test-takers. This definition is population-specific. If there is greater systematic variation in one population than another, such as in all public school students compared with only eighth-graders, the test will have greater reliability for the more varied population. This is a consequence of how reliability is defined. Reliability is a joint characteristic of a test and examinee group, not just a characteristic of a test. Indeed, reliability of any one test varies from group to group. Therefore, the better research studies will report the reliability for their sample as well as the reliability for norming groups as presented by the test publisher.

This chapter discusses sources of error, several approaches toward estimating reliability, and several ways to make tests more reliable.

Sources of Error

There are three major sources of error: factors in the test itself, factors in the students taking the test, and scoring factors.

Most tests contain a collection of items that represent particular skills. We typically generalize from each item to all items like it. For example, if a student can solve several problems like 7 times 8, then we may generalize his or her ability to multiply single-digit integers. We also generalize from the collection of items to a broader domain. If a student does well on a test of addition, subtraction, multiplication, and division of fractions, then we may generalize and conclude that the student is able to perform fraction operations. But error may be introduced by the selection of particular items to represent the skills and domains. The particular cross-section of test content included in the specific items on the test will vary with each test form, introducing sampling error and limiting the dependability of the test, since we are generalizing to unobserved data, namely, ability across all items that could have been on the test. On basic arithmetic skills, one would expect the content to be fairly similar, and thus building a highly reliable test is relatively easy. As the skills and domains become more complex, more errors are likely to be introduced by sampling of items. Other sources of test error include the effectiveness of the distractors (wrong options) in multiple choice tests, partially correct distractors, multiply correct answers, and the difficulty of the items relative to the student's ability.

As human beings, students are not always consistent and, hence, they also introduce error into the testing process. Whether a test is intended to measure typical or optimal student performance, changes in such things as student's attitudes, health, and sleep may affect the quality of his or her efforts and thus test-taking consistency. For example, test takers may make careless errors, misinterpret test instructions, forget test instructions, inadvertently omit test sections, or misread test items.

Scoring is a third potential source of error. On objective tests, the scoring is mechanical and scoring error should be minimal. On constructed response items, sources of error include lack of clarity in the scoring rubrics, lack of clarity in what is expected of the student, and a host of rater errors. Raters are not always consistent, sometimes change their criteria while scoring, and are subject to biases such as the halo effect, stereotyping, perception differences, leniency/stringency error, and scale shrinkage (see Rudner, 1992).

Measures of Reliability

It is impossible to calculate a reliability coefficient that conforms to the theoretical definition. Recall that the theoretical definition depends on knowing the degree to which a population of examinees vary in their true achievement (or whatever the test measures). But if we knew that degree of variance, then we wouldn't need the test! Instead, there are several statistics (coefficients) commonly used to estimate the stability of a set of test scores for a group of examinees: test-retest, split-half reliability, alternate-form reliability, and measures of internal consistency are the most common.

Test-retest reliability. A test-retest reliability coefficient is obtained by administering the same test twice and correlating the scores. In concept, it is an excellent measure of score consistency, because one is directly measuring consistency from administration to administration. This coefficient is not recommended in practice, however, because of its problems and limitations. It requires two administrations of the same test with the same group of indi-

> **Reliability is a joint characteristic of a test and examinee group.**

viduals. This is expensive and not a good use of people's time. If the time interval is short, people may be overly consistent because they remember some of the question and their responses. If the interval is long, then the results are confounded with learning and maturation, that is, changes in the test-takers themselves.

Split-half reliability. As the name suggests, split-half reliability is a coefficient obtained by dividing a test into halves, correlating the scores on each half, and then correcting for length (longer tests tend to be more reliable). The split can be based on odd versus even numbered items, randomly selecting items, or manually balancing content and difficulty. This approach has an advantage in that it only requires a single test administration. Its weakness is that the resultant coefficient will vary as a function of how the test was split. It is also not appropriate on tests where speed is a factor (that is, where students' scores are influenced by how many items they reach in the allotted time).

Internal consistency. Internal consistency focuses on the degree to which the individual items are correlated with each other and is thus often called homogeneity. Several statistics fall within this category. The best known are Cronbach's alpha, the Kuder-Richardson Formula 20 (KR-20) and the Kuder-Richardson Formula 21 (KR-21). Most testing programs that report data from one administration of a test to students do so using Cronbach's alpha, which is functionally equivalent to KR-20.

The advantages of these statistics are that they only require one test administration and that they do not depend on a particular split of items. The disadvantage is that they are most applicable when the test measures a single skill area.

Requiring only the test mean, standard deviation (or variance), and the number of items, the Kuder-Richardson formula 21, shown in Figure IV-1 is an extremely simple reliability formula. While it will almost always provide coefficients that are lower than KR-20, its simplicity makes it a very useful estimate of reliability, especially for evaluating some classroom-developed tests. It should not be used, however, if the test has items that are scored other than just zero or one.

Figure IV-1
The Kuder-Richardson Formula 21

$$KR21 = \frac{k}{k-1}\left(1 \; \frac{M(k-M)}{k\,\sigma^2}\right)$$

Where M is the mean, k is the number of items, and $k\,\sigma^2$ is the test variance.

Alternate-form reliability. Most standardized tests provide equivalent forms that can be used interchangeably. These alternative forms are typically matched in terms of content and difficulty. The correlation of scores on pairs of alternative forms for the same examinees provides another measure of consistency or reliability. Even with the best test and item specifications, each test would contain slightly different content and, as with test-retest reliability, maturation and learning may confound the results. The use of different items in the two forms, however, conforms to our goal of including the extent to which item sets contribute to random errors in estimating test reliability.

How High Should Reliability Be?

Most large-scale tests report reliability coefficients that exceed .80 and often exceed .90. The questions the test-giver should ask are: 1) What are the consequences of the test? and 2) Is the group used to compute the reported reliability like my group?

If the consequences are high, as in tests used for special education placement, high school graduation, or professional certification, then the internal consistency reliability needs to be quite high—at least above .90, preferably above .95. Misclassifications due to measurement error should be kept to a minimum. And please note that no test should ever be used by itself to make an important decision for anyone.

Classroom tests seldom need to have exceptionally high reliability coefficients. As more students master the content, test variability will go down and so will the coefficients from internal measures of reliability. Further, classroom tests don't need exceptionally high reliability coefficients. A teacher in the elementary grades sees the child all day and has gathered input from a variety of information sources. His or her knowledge and judgment, used along with information from the test, provides superior information. If a test is not reliable or it is not accurate for an individual, the teacher can and should make the appropriate corrections. A reliability coefficient of .50 or .60 may suffice.

Again, reliability is a joint characteristic of a test and examinee group, not just a characteristic of a test. Thus, reliability also needs to be evaluated in terms of the examinee group. A test with a reliability of .92 when administered to students in fourth, fifth, and sixth grades will not have as high a reliability when administered just to a group of fourth graders.

Improving Test Reliability

Developing better tests with less random measurement error is better than simply documenting the amount of error. Measurement error is reduced by writing items clearly, making the instructions easily understood, adhering to proper test administration, and scoring consistently. Because a test is a sample of the desired skills and behaviors, longer tests, which are larger samples, will be more reliable. A one-hour end-of-unit exam will be more reliable than a five-minute pop quiz. (Note that pop quizzes should be discouraged. By using them, a teacher is not only using assessments punitively, but is also missing the opportunity to capitalize on student preparation as an instructional activity.)

A Comment on Scoring

What does a teacher do if a child makes careless mistakes on a test? On one hand, the teacher wants his or her students to learn to follow directions, to think through their work, to check their work, and to be careful. On the other hand, tests are supposed to reflect what a student knows. Further, a low score due to careless mistakes is not the same as a low score due to lack of knowledge.

Especially in the elementary grades, a miserable test due to careless mistakes should not dramatically lower a student's grade for the semester. The semester grade should reflect what the student has achieved, since that is the meaning it will convey to others. We advocate keeping two sets of records, especially in the elementary grades, one set reflecting production, and the other reflecting achievement. The teacher then has the needed data to apply good judgment in conferencing with parents and for determining semester grades.

NORM- AND CRITERION-REFERENCED TESTING

By Linda A. Bond

Tests can be categorized into two major groups: norm-referenced tests and criterion-referenced tests. These two tests differ in their intended purposes, the way in which content is selected, and the scoring process that defines how the test results must be interpreted. This chapter describes the differences between these two types of assessment and explains the most appropriate uses of each.

Intended Purposes

The major reason for using a norm-referenced test (NRT) is to classify students. NRTs are designed to highlight achievement differences between and among students to produce a dependable rank order across a continuum of achievement from high to low achievers (Stiggins, 1994). School systems might want to classify students in this way so that they can be properly placed in remedial or gifted programs. These types of tests are also used to help teachers select students for different ability-level reading or mathematics instructional groups.

A representative group of students is given a norm-referenced test prior to its availability to the public. The scores of the students who take the test after publication are then compared to those of the norm group. Tests such as the California Achievement Test (CTB/McGraw-Hill), the Iowa Test of Basic Skills (Riverside), and the Metropolitan Achievement Test (Psychological Corporation) are normed using a national sample of students. Because norming a test is such an elaborate and expensive process, the norms are typically used by test publishers for seven years. All students who take the test during that seven-year period have their scores compared to the original norm group.

While norm-referenced tests ascertain the rank of students, criterion-referenced tests (CRTs) determine "...what test takers can do and what they know, not how they compare to others" (Anastasi, 1988, p. 102). CRTs report how well students are doing relative to a pre-determined performance level on a specified set of educational goals or outcomes included in the school, district, or state curriculum.

Educators or policy makers may choose to use a CRT when they wish to see how well students have learned the knowledge and skills they are expected to have mastered. The CRT results may be used as one piece of information to determine how well the student is learning and how well the school is teaching the desired curriculum.

Both NRTs and CRTs can be standardized. The Office of Technology Assessment of the U.S. Congress (1992) defines a standardized test as one that uses uniform procedures for administration and scoring in order to assure that the results from different people are comparable. Any kind of test—from multiple choice to essays to oral examinations—can be standardized if uniform scoring and administration are used (p. 165). This means that the comparison of student scores is possible. Thus, it can be assumed that two students who receive the identical scores on the same standardized test demonstrate corresponding levels of performance. Most national, state, and district tests are standardized so that every score can be interpreted in a uniform manner for all students and schools.

Selection of Test Content

Test content is an important factor when choosing between an NRT and a CRT. The content of an NRT is selected according to how well it ranks students from high achievers to low. The content of a CRT is determined by how well it matches the learning outcomes deemed most important. Although no test can measure everything of importance, the content of the CRT is selected on the basis of its significance in the curriculum, while that of the NRT is chosen by how well it discriminates among students.

Any national, state, or district test communicates to the public the skills that students should have acquired as well as the levels of student performance that are considered satisfactory. Therefore, education officials at any level should carefully consider content of the test that is selected or developed. Because of the importance placed upon high scores, the content of a standardized test can be very influential in the development of a school's curriculum and standards of excellence.

NRTs have come under attack recently because traditionally they have purported to focus on low-level basic skills. This emphasis is in direct contrast to the recommendations made by the latest research on teaching and learning which calls for educators to stress the acquisition of conceptual understanding as well as the application of skills. The National Council of Teachers of Mathematics (NCTM) has been particularly vocal about this concern. In an NCTM publication (1991), Romberg (1989) cited that "a recent study of the six most commonly used commercial achievement tests found that at grade 8, on average, only 1 percent of the items were problem solving while 77 percent were computation or estimation" (p. 8).

In order to best prepare their students for the standardized achievement tests, teachers usually devote much time to teaching the information found on the standardized tests. This is particularly true if the standardized tests are also used to measure an educator's teaching ability. The result of this pressure placed upon teachers for their students to perform well on these tests has resulted in an emphasis on low-level skills in the classroom (Corbett and Wilson, 1991). With curriculum specialists and educational policy makers alike calling for more attention to higher-level skills, these tests may be driving classroom practice in a direction opposite to that of educational reform.

Test Interpretation

As mentioned earlier, a student's performance on an NRT is interpreted in relation to the performance of a large group of similar students who took the test when it was first normed. For example, if a student receives a percentile rank score on the total test of 34, this means that he or she performed as well or better than 34 percent of the students in the norm group. This type of information can be useful for deciding whether or not students need remedial assistance or are candidates for a gifted program. The score, however, gives little information about what the student actually knows or can do.

Figure V-1
Appropriate Uses of Norm-referenced and Criterion-Referenced Tests*

PURPOSE	TEST	EXAMPLES	PRIMARY USERS
To compare achievement of local students to achievement of students in the nation, state, or other districts in a given year.	NRT	A comparison of achievement of local schools' 3rd graders to achievement of 3rd graders throughout the nation.	Central office, (including school boards), parents
To compare achievement of subgroups of local students to achievement of similar subgroups in the nation, state, or other districts in a given year.	NRT	A comparison of achievement of local black students to the achievement of black students throughout the nation.	Central office
To compare achievement of one local school's student subgroup (e.g. sex, race, or age) to achievement of another such subgroup in a given year to determine the equity of educational outcomes.	NRT	A comparison of achievement of black and white students in local schools to determine and monitor any gap in achieve-ment.	Central office, principals
To assess the extent to which students in a single grade level (at district, building, or classroom level) have mastered the essential objectives of the school system's curriculum.	CRT	A comparison of difference between results of September and May criterion-referenced tests to determine the extent to which 3rd graders at a given school attained 3rd grade objectives in reading.	Teachers, principals, central office
To assess the extent to which a given student is learning the essential objectives of the school system's curriculum and, subsequently, to adjust instruction for that student.	CRT	The use of the results from the September and January criter-ion-referenced tests as one indicator to help determine if a student is properly placed in an instruc-tional group.	Teachers, principals, parents
To track achievement of cohort of students through the system or area to determine the extent to which their achievement improves over time.	CRT	An examination of progress of all 3rd graders in system, administra-tive area, or school from one year to the next.	Central office, principals
To track achievement of cohort of students in a given school to determine the extent to which they learn essential objectives of school system's curriculum as they go from grade to grade.	CRT	The use of May criterion-referenced tests (or perhaps gains from September to May), to follow the progress of children over time in terms of the extent to which they learned the curriculum from one year to another.	Principals, teachers

*This chart was prepared by Prince George's County (Maryland) Public Schools.

The validity of the score in these decision processes depends on whether or not the content of the NRT matches the knowledge and skills expected of the students in that particular school system.

It is easier to ensure the match to expected skills with a CRT. CRTs give detailed information about how well a student has performed on each of the educational goals or outcomes included on that test. For instance, "... a CRT score might describe which arithmetic operations a student can perform or the level of reading difficulty he or she can comprehend" (U.S. Congress, OTA, 1992, p. 170). As long as the content of the test matches the content considered important to learn, the CRT gives the student, the teacher, and the parent more information than an NRT does about how much of the valued content has been learned.

The chart in Figure V-1 represents the approach of one county to the appropriate uses of norm-referenced and criterion-referenced tests.

Summary

Public demands for accountability, and consequently for high standardized test scores, are not going to disappear. In 1994, only 31 states administered NRTs, while 33 administered CRTs. Among these states, 22 administered both. Only two states rely on NRTs exclusively, while one state relies exclusively on a CRT. Acknowledging the recommendations for educational reform and the popularity of standardized tests, some states are designing tests that "reflect, insofar as possible, what we believe to be appropriate educational practice" (NCTM, 1991, p .9). In addition to this, most states also administer other forms of assessment such as a writing sample, some form of open-ended performance assessment, or a portfolio (CCSSO/NCREL, 1994).

Before a state can choose what type of standardized test to use, the state education officials will have to consider if that test meets three standards. These criteria are: whether the assessment strategies of a particular test match the state's educational goals, address the content the state wishes to assess, and allow the kinds of interpretations state education officials wish to make about student performance. Once they have determined these three things, the task of choosing between the NRT and CRT will become easier.

VI.

SOME MEASUREMENT CONCEPTS

By Lawrence M. Rudner

What Types of Test Scores Are There?

Different types of scores provide different types of information and serve different purposes. You should understand the different types of scores before you try to use them or select scores that are most appropriate for your needs.

In the first part of this chapter, the following types of test scores are defined:

- raw scores

- total percent correct scores

- objective percent correct scores

- percentile scores (ranks)

- stanine scores

- grade equivalent scores

- standard scores

- normal curve equivalent scores

and the advantages and disadvantages of each are explained. The uses of each are discussed at the end of the chapter.

Remember that test scores reflect only what has been measured on a particular test (the test domain). For example, scores on the Iowa Test of Basic

Skills (ITBS) for mathematics achievement reflect only the combination of skills tested by that ITBS. Scores on other mathematics tests are comparable to the extent that their domains are comparable.

Raw Scores

Raw scores indicate the number of items a student answers correctly on a test. For students who take the same test, it makes sense to compare their raw scores. If one third grade student answers 12 of 25 items correctly and another answers 16 correctly, then we are likely to conclude that the second student knows the content of that test better than the first.

Because the number of items varies between tests and because tests vary in difficulty, raw scores have little value in making comparisons from one subject to another. Suppose a third grade student answers 12 out of 25 items correctly on a mathematics test and 16 out of 25 items on a reading test. Some people may assume that the student is better in reading than in mathematics. However, we really know nothing about relative performance in the two different areas because the mathematics test may be much harder than the reading test.

How are raw scores distributed?

As an example of how raw scores are usually distributed over the population, let's look at a national sample of 2,000 students.

If you give a 25-item mathematics test to a large number of students, you will typically find the largest number have scores around the average, or mean, and the number of students with a given raw score decreases the further you get from the mean. Figure VI-1 illustrates a hypothetical number of students with each test score.

The distribution of test scores shown in Figure VI-1 can be modeled mathematically using the familiar bell-shaped normal curve.

In the normal curve shown in Figure VI-2, the y (vertical) axis shows the relative proportion of students and the x (horizontal) axis shows the total raw score. The curve is used to approximate the proportion of students who would have a given total score.

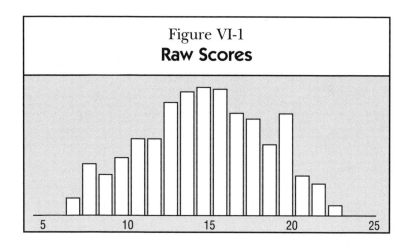

Figure VI-1
Raw Scores

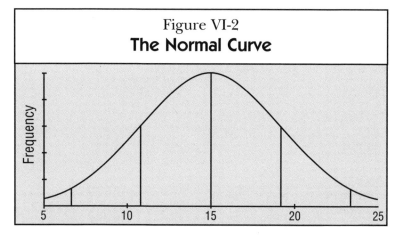

Figure VI-2
The Normal Curve

The normal curve is only a mathematical model that shows a relationship between two variables—test scores and proportion of students. Actual scores never perfectly match the model. Nevertheless, the model is close to reality and gives good practical results. The same relationship between test scores and proportion of students holds for a wide number of tests.

Test developers use the model of the normal curve in developing and norming tests. In this guide, we use it to show similarities between different types of normative test scores—test scores that describe individual student performance in comparison to the actual performance of a large group of students.

Two statistics are helpful in discussing test score distributions:

- the *mean*
- the *standard deviation.*

The *mean* is frequently called the average score. You compute the mean by adding all the scores, then dividing the sum by the total number of scores.

A *deviation* score is *how far away the score is from the mean.* For example, on a test with a mean of 15, a score of 20 deviates 5 points from the mean. The deviation score alone does not tell you whether this is a big difference or not. Rather, the standard deviation gives you a framework for interpreting this test score variability. You compute the standard deviation by taking the square root of the average of all the squared deviations. You can interpret standard deviation as an average distance that the scores deviate from the mean.

What are the advantages of raw scores?

- They are easy to compute.
- One of the most accurate ways to analyze a student's gains in achievement is to compare the raw scores from two administrations of the same test.

What is the limitation of raw scores?

Raw scores do not contain a frame of reference for indicating how well a student is performing.

Total Percent Correct Scores

Total percent correct scores tell you the percentage of items that a student answers correctly out of the total number of items on a test. Like raw scores, total percent correct scores do not reflect varying degrees of item and test difficulty. They are of limited value in making comparisons.

Note that total percent correct scores are NOT the same as percentile scores. (We discuss percentile scores later in this section.)

What are the advantages of total percent correct scores?

- They are easy to compute.

- They adjust for differing numbers of items.

What are the limitations of total percent correct scores?

- They do not adjust for differing test difficulties.

- They do not contain a frame of reference for indicating how well a student is performing.

- They can mislead teachers, students, and others into thinking the percent correct a student receives is the percent of the content the student knows or can do.

Objective Percent Correct Scores

Objective percent correct scores tell you the percent of the items measuring a single objective that a student answers correctly. Because objectives and items can vary in difficulty, this score is of limited value for determining whether a student has mastered a learning objective. Indeed, the objective percent correct score is really a percent correct score for a reduced test domain (that is, one reduced to a single objective).

You might interpret the objective percent correct score in relation to an *expected* objective percent correct. Expectations are sometimes based on curricular goals, last year's performance, or national averages. But, since different collections of test items will not be equivalent in difficulty, comparing one student's objective percent correct with another student's—or with an expectation—should only be done when the items are identical or equivalent.

Expectations can be used to convert objective percent correct scores to *objective mastery scores*. When the expectation is met or exceeded, the *objective is mastered*. Conversely, when the score is lower than expected, the objective is not mastered.

For example, suppose a test contains eight whole-number addition problems and a student answers seven of them correctly. That student's objective percent correct score is 87.5 percent. If you feel that answering, say, three out of every four questions correctly reflects mastery, then this test score indicates that the student has mastered the objective.

What are the advantages of objective mastery scores?

- They are easy to compute.

- They adjust for differing numbers of items per objective.

- They help you diagnose specific individual strengths and weaknesses.

- They provide a skill-based approach to classroom grouping and school-based curricular emphasis.

What are the limitations of objective mastery scores?

- They require a fairly large number of items (usually more than 10) for each objective.

- The fewer items there are per objective, the greater is the likelihood of mistaking masters from non-masters and vice versa.

- Expectations are not always easy to define. The national average is not always a good basis for determining expectation.

- They do not indicate the degree or level of skill that the student has attained; they only indicate the status of mastery or non-mastery.

Percentile Scores (ranks)

Percentile scores tell you the percent of students in the norming sample whose scores are at or lower than a given score. Percentile scores are among the most commonly reported scores and are best used to describe a student's standing in relation to the norming group at the time of testing. For example, if a student's score is in the 80th percentile, then that student has scored equal to or higher than 80 percent of the students who took the test when the test was normed.

Note that although percentile scores are reported in increments of one hundredths, they are not completely accurate. When you use percentiles, you should pay attention to the *confidence bands* that the test publisher provides.

Confidence bands represent the *range of scores* in which a student's true score is likely to fall. For example, although a student's score on a particular test may be at the 86th percentile, it is likely that if the student took the same test on a different day, the new score would vary slightly. Accounting for random variations, that student's true achievement may fall somewhere within a range of scores, for example, between the 81st and 89th percentiles.

Percentile units are used to report an individual student's score; they should not be averaged to describe groups. Percentile units cannot be subtracted to compute gains because differences in percentile scores are not constant across the entire scale. For example, getting an additional two items correct can greatly increase a percentile rank for an average student. Yet the score increase from the same two items may not result in any percentile change for students who achieve far above average. Score gains increase percentile ranks more in the middle of the range than toward the extremes. (See Figure VI-3.)

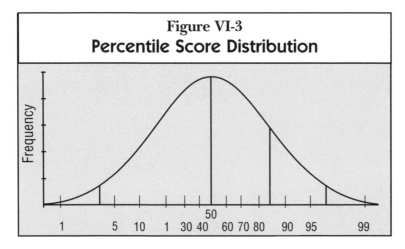

Figure VI-3
Percentile Score Distribution

How are percentile scores distributed?

Figure VI-3 shows how percentile scores are distributed when raw scores are distributed normally. The y (vertical) axis shows the proportion of students and the x (horizontal) axis shows the percentile score. Vertical lines have been drawn to indicate each standard deviation unit. Note that the percentile scores are not evenly distributed on the x-axis. If they were evenly distributed, then the proportions graphed on the y-axis would all be the same; each proportion would be 1 percent!

Notice that percentiles are wider apart at the ends of the figure. For example, the raw score difference between the 95th and 90th percentile is greater than the difference between the 55th and 50th. This happens because a student needs to answer more items correctly to move from the 90th to the 95th percentile than is necessary to move from the 50th to 55th percentile. Therefore, scores are clustered around the mean. It is because of this difference that you should not add, subtract, or average percentiles.

What are the advantages of percentile scores?
- They show how students rank in relation to the national or local average.

- They are easy to explain.

What are the limitations of percentile scores?
- They can be confused with total percent correct scores.

- They are not as accurate as they appear to be.

- They are often used inappropriately to compute group statistics or to determine gains.

- They are frequently misunderstood.

Stanine Scores

Stanine is short for standard nine. Stanine scores range from a low of 1 to a high of 9 with:

- 1, 2, or 3 representing below average

- 4, 5, or 6 representing average

- 7, 8, or 9 representing above average.

If a student achieves a stanine score that is below average in a particular area, the test has revealed an area in which the student may need to improve—or at least it reveals an area in which the student is weak when compared to other students who have taken the test. If the student achieves an average stanine score, the test has revealed that the student performed at the same level as most of the other students who took the test. Similarly, if the student achieves a stanine score that is above average, the test has revealed that the student performed better in that area than most of the other students who took the test.

Stanines are frequently used as a basis for grouping students. For example, an advanced mathematics class may enroll students in the 9th, 8th, and sometimes 7th stanine.

How are stanine scores distributed?

Figure VI-4 shows how stanine scores are distributed when raw scores are distributed normally. The y (vertical) axis shows the proportion of students and the x (horizontal) axis shows the stanine score. Vertical lines have been drawn to indicate each standard deviation unit. Stanine 5 represents one-half of a standard deviation (sd) around the mean. Stanines 2, 3, 4 and 6, 7, 8 also represent the same raw score difference (1/2 sd). Stanines 1 and 9 represent all the scores below -1.75 sd and above +1.75 sd, respectively.

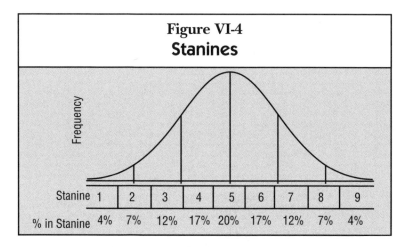

Stanine scores are normalized. This means they will be distributed normally whether or not the original test was normally distributed. This is accomplished by assigning the highest and lowest 4 percent of the test scores to stanine 9 and 1, respectively; the next highest and lowest 7 percent to stanines 8 and 2; the next highest and lowest 12 percent to stanines 7 and 3, the next highest and lowest 17 percent to stanines 6 and 4, and the middle 20 percent to stanine 5. The percentages were chosen to approximate a normal distribution.

District test results can be reported by showing the percent of district students who fall in each stanine computed based on a national norming group.

What are the advantages of stanine scores?

- They show the standing of students in relation to the national or local average.

- They are relatively easy to explain.

- They can be used to group students into ability groups.

What are the limitations of stanine scores?

- They should not be used in computing group statistics or in determining gains.

- They give only very general indications of a student's relative standing in a particular content area.

Grade Equivalent Scores

Grade equivalent scores use a scale based on grade levels and months to estimate how well students perform. These scores reflect the median score of students across several grade levels during the month the test was normed. For instance, the median test score for first graders in the seventh month of the school year (April) would convert to a score of 1.7, for second graders the score would be 2.7, for third graders the score would be 3.7, and so forth.

Grade equivalent scores are often misunderstood. For example, if a fourth grader received a grade equivalent score of 7.0 on a fourth grade reading achievement test, some people may assume that the fourth grader has mastered seventh grade material. However, the score actually means that the fourth grader reads fourth grade material as well as the typical beginning seventh grader (in September) would read the same fourth grade material.

As with percentile scores, you should use grade equivalent scores only to describe a student's standing in relation to the norming group at the time of testing. You should not average grade equivalent scores to describe groups, and you should not subtract them to compute gains.

As with differences in percentile scores, differences in grade equivalent scores do not mean the same thing across the entire scale.

How are grade equivalent scores distributed?

Figure VI-5 shows an example of how grade equivalent scores are distributed when raw scores are distributed normally. The y (vertical) axis shows the proportion of students and the x (horizontal) axis shows the grade equivalents. Vertical lines have been drawn to indicate each standard deviation unit. (Note that this is just an example, because grade equivalent scores are not defined by the model but rather by the actual performance on the test by students in higher and lower grade levels.)

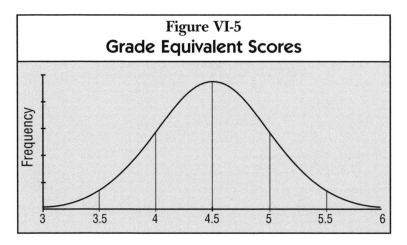

Figure VI-5
Grade Equivalent Scores

Notice that relatively few correct responses translate to large differences in grade equivalent scores for students who achieve very high and very low scores. Because of this, grade equivalent scores do not estimate group ability well, and you should not use them to evaluate gains over time.

What is the advantage of grade equivalent scores?
- Grade equivalent scores are expressed in grade-level values that are familiar to parents and teachers.

What are the limitations of grade equivalent scores?
- They are frequently misunderstood and misinterpreted.

- They have low accuracy for students who have very high or very low scores.

- They should not be used for computing group statistics or in determining gains.

Standard Scores

Standard scores tell you how much students' scores deviate from a mean. Almost all of the companies that publish achievement tests will give you standard scores. However, they often use different names—such as *growth scale values, developmental standard scores,* and *scaled scores*—and different units to report the scores. Thus, a scaled score of 110 on one test may not be the same as a scaled score of 110 on another.

The main advantage of standard scores is that they give you an equal interval unit of measurement. As a result, you can use them to compute summary statistics, such as averages and gains, if all the students you compare took the same test. A two-point difference between standard scores means the same difference, no matter where a student falls within the range of scores (unlike percentile and grade equivalent scores).

As we noted, the scales used for standard scores differ among test publishers and among content areas. As a result, you cannot usually use these scores to compare results on different tests.

How are standard scores distributed?

Figure VI-6 shows how standard scores are distributed on a hypothetical test when raw scores are distributed normally. Here the raw scores have been translated to a scale with a mean of 100 and a standard deviation of 10. The y (vertical) axis shows the proportion of students and the x (horizontal) axis shows the standard score. Vertical lines have been drawn to indicate each standard deviation unit.

Note that the intervals in Figure VI-6 are equal in size. This feature makes standard scores and scores based on standard scores the statistic of choice when reporting group averages and changes over time.

What are the advantages of standard scores?

- They are linearly related to raw scores and thus have many of the advantages of raw scores.

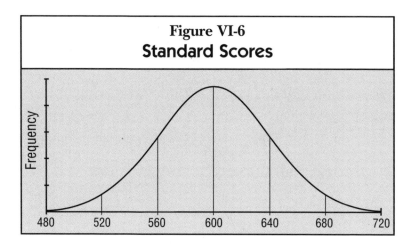

Figure VI-6
Standard Scores

Frequency

480   520   560   600   640   680   720

- They show relative performance of a student within a group.

What are the limitations of standard scores?

- They can be confusing to parents and teachers unless they are converted to percentile scores.

- They have no intrinsic meaning, unless the scale is commonly understood because it is used frequently. For example, the Scholastic Aptitude Test (SAT) for college admissions uses a standard score with a mean of 500 and a standard deviation of 100.

Normal Curve Equivalent Scores

Normal curve equivalent scores were originally developed to analyze and report gains in compensatory programs for educationally disadvantaged students. These scores have a mean of 50 and a standard deviation of approximately 21. This results in a scale with 99 equal interval units.

A normal curve equivalent score of 50 represents the national average of any grade level at the time of year the test was normed. A score of 30 is always the same distance below grade level, regardless of the level tested, and is twice as far below grade level as a score of 40.

Normal curve equivalent scores are similar in their range to percentile scores, but they have statistical properties that allow them to be used to compute summary statistics and gain scores.

How are normal curve equivalent scores distributed?

Normal curve equivalents are normalized scores (see the discussion of stanines above). Figure VI-7 shows how normal curve equivalent scores are distributed. The y (vertical) axis shows the proportion of students and the x (horizontal) axis shows the score. Vertical lines have been drawn to indicate each standard deviation unit.

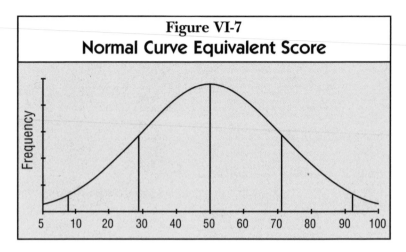

Figure VI-7
Normal Curve Equivalent Score

Because normal curve equivalents are a type of standard score, they have the same statistical properties as standard scores. Normal curve equivalent intervals are of equal size and these scores can be used to compute group statistics.

What are the advantages of normal curve equivalent scores?

- They allow you to compare the performance of students who take different levels or forms of the same test within a test battery.

- They allow you to draw comparisons across subject matter for the same student.

- They can be used to evaluate gains over time.

- They can be used to combine data from different tests.

- They can be used to compute meaningful summary statistics.

What is the limitation of normal curve equivalent scores?

Normal curve equivalent scores do not give you easily understood information about an individual student's achievement level unless they are compared to another value or are converted to a percentile score.

How Should You Use Test Scores?

Interpreting Norm-Referenced Test Scores

Normative test scores—stanines, percentile scores, scaled scores, and grade equivalent scores—measure an *individual* student's achievement in relation to the achievement of *one or more large groups* of students who took the same test. The comparison group may be composed of other students in your district or of students from a nationally representative sample. Thus, scores on norm-referenced tests are meaningful only in relation to a comparison group.

Your school or district is not completely like the normative group. No district is. In many cases, the differences are minor and inconsequential. In other cases, however, schools can be so different that the national norms provided by the publisher do not accurately reflect school performance. Norms become less meaningful as your students and your testing program become more unlike the standardization sample.

If your students are tested at a different time of the year than the norm group was tested, the interpretation of the percentile score is unclear. For example, the California Achievement Test (CAT) is normed in October. That means that you must give it in October to make your students' scores most meaningful. If you give the CAT in January, you cannot know if a student who scores in the 55th percentile is above or below average when compared to grade-level peers.

Many of these differences can seriously affect your scores. This does not mean the national norms are useless; it means that you must evaluate the norms in perspective. Some publishers extrapolate norms so they are based on the week the test was given, for example. Norms give you an index of how well students perform on certain tasks—tasks the test publishers have identified as representing the skills taught to the comparison group at the time the test was developed.

Norm groups are used at varying points in time, but their data are actually historical. Scores that are above average, for example, may be only above the average of students in the norm group who were tested four years ago. They may not be above today's average for a similarly defined group.

The comparative baseline of norm-referenced tests is a powerful tool. In addition to worrying whether your chapter 1 students are learning basic skills, for example, you probably are also interested in how well they are doing in relation to the nation. Although your students may not be like the nation at large, they are going to be competing for jobs and educational opportunities against a wide range of other students.

While national averages give you a baseline, you must establish your own expectations and goals considering your particular community and curriculum. For example, it would be somewhat misleading for you to report above average scores for a magnet school that selects students based on academic achievement. In this case, you would be better off reporting on the gains or specific achievements of the students who are in the program.

VII.

USING STATE STANDARDS AND ASSESSMENTS TO IMPROVE INSTRUCTION

By Christopher Tienken and Michael Wilson

Today many states around the country have curriculum standards, and state-developed assessments to monitor the implementation of those standards. Most state standards define expected outcomes—that is, what students need to know and be able to do—but do not mandate specific strategies or pedagogy to be used by local districts. Elementary, middle, and high school students around the country take at least one state-mandated test during their school career. However, 35 out of 50 states do not require teachers to take a course, or demonstrate competency, in the area of assessment. Hence, teachers generally have limits to their knowledge of how to design and use tests and assessment tools. Richard Stiggins (1999) wrote, "It is time to rethink the relationship between assessment and effective schooling."

It is possible for teachers and administrators to use state content and process standards, test specifications, curriculum frameworks, sample questions, educational research, and exemplar papers to improve instruction and classroom tests and assessment procedures, but limited understanding puts constraints on this use. Researchers Paul Black and Dylan Wiliam (1998) have stated that standards are raised only by changing what happens in the classroom, beginning with teachers and students. These researchers go on to say that a large body of evidence suggests that attention to formative assessment is a vital feature of classroom work and the development of it can raise standards.

This chapter describes a program used by two educators to help teachers improve instruction through a deeper understanding of state standards and test specifications. Any teacher or administrator in any state can use the process outlined in this chapter. Specific examples were developed using the New Jersey Core Curriculum Content Standards and that state's fourth grade mathematics test.

Developing a Knowledge Base

Understanding how standards-based state tests are constructed is the first step in being able to use them to guide and improve instruction. A test is essentially a sample of questions or activities that reflect a large body of knowledge and mental processes associated with an academic subject area. It is highly impractical to design a test that includes all of the problems that a student could ever do in each content area. Therefore, state tests are samples of possible questions from each area. All state tests are limited samples of what students are required to know in areas such as language arts, mathematics, science, etc. Such large numbers of questions could appear on future forms of these instruments that a teacher would not be able to address all the possible questions, nor should she or he attempt that task. School districts and teachers, however, should endeavor to understand the delineation of each subject area.

School districts are under pressure to perform well on state tests and often use a test preparation strategy of giving students sample tests from commercially prepared workbooks or state released items to get ready for state tests. Although this strategy can be useful for providing general information regarding student strengths and weaknesses as related to the samples, it should not be the only method used by teachers. Such preparation for testing does little to educate teachers about how to use and understand state tests, standards, and test specifications. This chapter recommends a three-part process for developing an understanding of state assessments and using that understanding to improve instruction. That process is delineation, alignment, and calibration.

Delineation

Delineation is the first component needed for understanding any standards-based test. It is the process of thoroughly identifying all aspects of a particular subject domain; the aspects are also known as *dimensions*. Delineation involves the use of state testing documents that describe each content area of the assessment. These documents usually include test specifications, specific skill cluster information, subject area frameworks, assessment examples and exemplars, and the state standards. Delineation requires an examination of the documents for assessment dimensions such as content, cognitive level, and complexity. A thorough delineation might also include analysis of the test format, motivation, the difficulty level of the questions, and related affective characteristics of the subject area.

Thoroughly examining state standards and test specifications is a way to begin delineation. The New Jersey Standards include macro or big-picture statements and cumulative progress indicators that provide details about general performance expectations. The state's test specifications are particularly helpful because they go further and break the Standards down into two distinct types. Knowledge specifications describe the specific processes and content that all students must know by the end of fourth grade. Some would call these *content standards*. Problem solving specifications describe what students should be able to do with the content knowledge. They are also known as *process standards*. Figure VII-1 contains an example excerpted from the fourth grade New Jersey mathematics standards and test specification manuals.

Figure VII-1
Fourth Grade Math Standards (New Jersey)

Macro Standard 4.1: All students will develop the ability to pose and solve mathematical problems in mathematics, other disciplines, and everyday experiences.

Cumulative Progress Indicator 4.1.2: Recognize, formulate, and solve problems arising from mathematical situations and everyday experiences.

Test Specification Manual - Cluster IV Discrete Mathematics:
Knowledge (content standards): Students should have a conceptual understanding of: Tree diagram

Problem Solving (process standards): In problem solving settings, students should be able to: Draw and interpret networks and tree diagrams

---

After reviewing the fourth grade New Jersey Core Curriculum Content Standards and test specifications for mathematics, a teacher would be able to identify seven distinct mathematics strands or dimensions. Those strands are:

- numeration and number theory
- whole number operations
- fractions and decimals
- measurement/time/money
- geometry
- probability/statistics
- pre-algebra.

Figure VII-2 represents the content delineation of the domain of mathematics after a team of fourth-grade teachers examined the New Jersey Core Curriculum Content Standards, fourth-grade state test specifications, and the local curriculum.

Figure VII-2
BA Delineation of the Domain of Mathematics

Mathematics Domain

Numeration/Number Theory	Whole Number Operations
Fractions/Decimals	Measurement/Time/Money
Geometry	Pre-algebra
Probability/Statistics	

(Delineated Strands / Dimensions)

Working through the different dimensions associated with the delineation process helps to increase teacher and administrator understanding of each content area and its relationship to the standards, classroom instruction, and assessment.

The following activities can begin once teachers and administrators specify all of the subject area dimensions:

- selecting and designing classroom assessments and practice questions

- revising and designing curriculum that is congruent with the content identified in the state standards and the district's delineation of the state-designed exams

- designing teacher training using instructional techniques that support these dimensions

A closer look at the fourth-grade New Jersey Core Curriculum Content Standards and test specifications for mathematics reveals an emphasis on performance and the use of mathematics to solve open-ended and word problems. The test specifications for that exam imply that the mathematics test questions are primarily composed of problem solving tasks. Therefore, it is safe to assume that test questions will require thinking in the application, analysis, and perhaps synthesis and evaluation levels of cognition.

Alignment

During the alignment phase, administrators and teachers work to identify, analyze, generalize, and describe the links between the various elements associated with the subject area previously delineated and the sample questions selected for practice or classroom activities to assess student progress. The sample questions and student assessments can be derived from several sources including state-released test items, commercially manufactured test preparation materials, or teacher made activities. Teachers and administrators examine linkages in the materials, organization, textbooks, instructional strategies, and other elements described in the curricula and used in daily instructional activities to ensure consistency with the district's delineation of the state assessment.

Using and understanding the test specifications become even more important at this stage. Let's imagine that a pair of fourth-grade teachers recently completed a delineation of the mathematics domain and identified their next unit of study. The unit centered on Standard 4.1.1 and the test specification shown in Figure VIII-3. Reviewing the example from the test specification manual and Cluster IV the teacher would complete several alignment tasks.

Figure VII-3
Test Specification Manual—
Cluster IV Discrete Mathematics:

Knowledge (content standards): Students should have a conceptual understanding of: Tree diagram

Problem Solving (process standards): In problem solving settings, students should be able to: Draw and interpret networks and tree diagrams

Tasks:

1. Review classroom resources, curriculum, textbooks, teacher activities, student thinking strategies, and tests to ensure that the above test specifications and macro standards are addressed on the knowledge and problem solving level. Do the teacher resource materials and classroom instruction address the proper skills?

2. Review the above factors to ensure congruency between the level of difficulty required by the standards and specifications, and the difficulty of the actual teacher resources and activities. Do the teacher's tests, lessons, activities, etc., match the difficulty level required by the standards and specifications?

3. The teacher must also consider format. Although less important than skills and difficulty, the teacher resources, activities, and tests should familiarize the students with state test question formats.

4. Teachers must align classroom assignments and activities to the subject area delineation to ensure congruency.

Calibration

After completing the delineation and beginning the alignment processes, *calibration* begins. Calibration is the act of conducting communications and interactions with teaching staff based on the information identified in delineation and used in alignment. The calibration process ensures that the conceptualization of content, cognitive process, complexity, formats, etc. is consistently understood for each subject area. Calibration, in its simplest form, is designing classroom instruction, activities, and assessments that are congruent with content area delineation and alignment. Using the prior mathematics vignette as an example, one can begin to see how the process takes place. Figure VII-4 represents the sequence of events leading up to calibration.

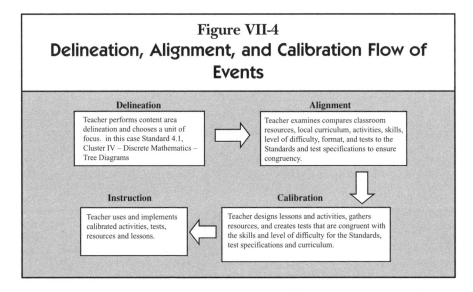

Figure VII-4

Delineation, Alignment, and Calibration Flow of Events

Delineation
Teacher performs content area delineation and chooses a unit of focus. in this case Standard 4.1, Cluster IV – Discrete Mathematics – Tree Diagrams

Alignment
Teacher examines compares classroom resources, local curriculum, activities, skills, level of difficulty, format, and tests to the Standards and test specifications to ensure congruency.

Instruction
Teacher uses and implements calibrated activities, tests, resources and lessons.

Calibration
Teacher designs lessons and activities, gathers resources, and creates tests that are congruent with the skills and level of difficulty for the Standards, test specifications and curriculum.

Imagine that a fourth grade-teacher completed delineation and alignment and discovered that his or her program was missing a unit on discrete mathematics. That teacher would develop objectives related to understanding, using, and interpreting tree diagrams. Figure VII-5 is a sample activity/test question created by fourth-grade teacher Terry Maher to begin addressing the aspect of discrete math noted in the Cluster IV test specification.

Calibration is any action that helps teachers design activities and construct assessments based on the dimensions of state assessments and standards. This process helps to foster a collective understanding of and agreement on the

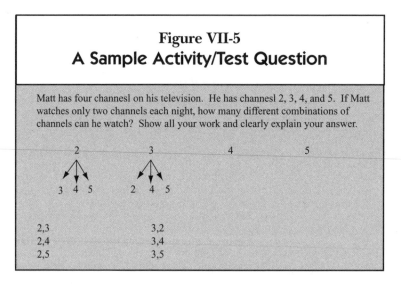

Figure VII-5
A Sample Activity/Test Question

Matt has four channesl on his television. He has channesl 2, 3, 4, and 5. If Matt watches only two channels each night, how many different combinations of channels can he watch? Show all your work and clearly explain your answer.

2   3   4   5

3 4 5   2 4 5

2,3	3,2
2,4	3,4
2,5	3,5

dimensions and domains of each content area. It should be a team effort based on group inquiry.

Using Score Reports to Improve Calibration

As teachers gain a better understanding of how student work reflects the standards and test specifications through delineation, alignment, and calibration, their efficiency and accuracy at identifying which students are meeting the standards should increase. Herein lies the usefulness of score reports. State test score reports sort students into categories of varying proficiency. For example, a student who scores partially proficient, proficient, or advanced proficient on a state language arts test may also show some congruency in the level of achievement in his or her well-aligned school work and classroom assessments. As teachers become better calibrated, they will be able to answer questions such as: Is the student showing partial proficiency, proficiency, or advanced proficiency on class assessments? If not, why? Is the difficulty level of the class work comparable to the state exam? What can I do to help this student meet the state standards? Is my program meeting the standards?

Predicting Outcomes

Teachers can reflect upon their level of calibration accuracy by attempting to predict student results on state assessments. This type of exercise acts as an extension to the calibration process and can provide teachers with a way to get a very general sense of their level of calibration. Teachers should be aware that there would not be 100 percent agreement between a student's performance on well-calibrated classroom tests and state assessments based on many factors of test design. Predicting outcomes is meant to complement the calibration exercises and provide the teacher with extra data regarding their calibration exercises.

To begin the prediction process, the teacher uses a list of the students taking the test. Beside each name, he or she enters a predicted score level. When the state assessment scores arrive, the teacher can compute the level of accuracy as shown below.

Name	Prediction	Score
Allan	Proficient	Adv. Proficient
Ann	Proficient	Proficient
Tamika	Adv. Proficient	Proficient
Bronson	Partial Proficient	Partial Proficient

The list above shows a 50 percent level of success in the predictions made. The teacher making the predictions returns to each student's work and compares the successful predictions with the unsuccessful ones to gain a better idea of how the assessment performances reflect the aligned student work. Student work associated with actual test scores can form the basis for subsequent calibration discussions. Student work connected to state assessment score levels can also function as scoring examples the students can refer to when judging their own level of achievement.

Final Thoughts

The process outlined in this chapter is very different from the idea of using testing materials and example tests to teach specific items on state assessments. Although there is a place for such strategies, this chapter suggests that it is more important for the teacher to understand the entirety of each subject area, and where state test content fits within each of these areas. Teachers must teach toward an understanding of the subject areas while they align and calibrate their classroom activities, resources, tests, and instruction with the specifications and skills required by each state's standards. There is a distinct difference between traditional notions of test preparation and aligning and calibrating instruction and assessments with the content, cognition, difficulty, and format of state assessment instruments, specifications, and standards. The aim is to ensure that teachers understand, and calibrate their classroom teaching with respect to the entire process and not simply focus on how to answer specific types of test questions.

The questions will change, but the underlying skills and concepts will not. One must be careful not to wallow in the mire of test prep. As educators, we are trying to link the classroom activities to the standards and skills set by the state. Delineation, alignment, and calibration are academic endeavors that demand unending commitment. Do not expect to accomplish alignment or calibration at an in-service day, or even during the course of a school year. This ongoing process requires constant attention. The administration must provide the time and resources to conduct frequent calibration meetings to examine such issues as classroom work and student assessment samples. Always beware—it is easy to fall out of alignment and calibration and into test prep.

VIII.

PREPARING STUDENTS TO TAKE STANDARDIZED ACHIEVEMENT TESTS

By William A. Mehrens

The public often favors accountability in education and believes that holding teachers responsible for students' achievement will result in better education. Many people believe that the best data about students' levels of achievement come from standardized achievement tests. Although scores from these tests are undoubtedly useful for accountability purposes, educators recognize that such data have some limitations.

Teaching to the Test

One major concern about standardized achievement tests is that when test scores are used to make important decisions, teachers may teach too directly to the test. Although teaching to the test is not a new concern, today's greater emphasis on teacher accountability can make this practice more likely to occur.

Depending on how it is done, teaching to the test can be either productive or counterproductive. Therefore, you need to carefully consider how you prepare students to take standardized achievement tests.

At some point, legitimate teaching to the test can cross an ill-defined line and become inappropriate teaching of the test (Shepard and Kreitzer, 1987). Educators may disagree about what specific activities are inappropriate. Therefore, it may be useful to describe a continuum of appropriateness and identify several points located on it.

Seven Points on the Continuum

Mehrens and Kaminski (1989) suggest the following descriptive points:

1. giving general instruction on district objectives without referring to the objectives that the standardized tests measure

2. teaching test-taking skills

3. providing instruction on objectives where objectives may have been determined by looking at the objectives that a variety of standardized tests measure (The objectives taught may or may not contain objectives on teaching test-taking skills.)

4. providing instruction based on objectives (skills and subskills) that specifically match those on the standardized test to be administered

5. providing instruction on specifically matched objectives (skills and subskills) where the practice or instruction follows the same format as the test questions

6. providing practice or instruction on a published parallel form of the same test

7. providing practice or instruction on the test itself

Mehrens and Kaminski suggest that:

- Point 1 is always ethical and Points 6 and 7 are never ethical.

- Point 2 is typically considered ethical.

Thus, the point at which you cross over from a legitimate to an illegitimate practice on the continuum is somewhere between Points 3 and 5. The location of the point changes, depending on the inferences you want to make from the test scores.

What You Can Infer from Test Scores

The only reasonable, direct inference you can make from a test score is the degree to which a student knows the content that the test samples. Any inference about why the student knows that content to that degree...is clearly a weaker inference.... (Mehrens, 1984, p. 10).

Teaching to the test alters what you can interpret from test scores because it involves teaching specific content. Therefore, it also weakens the direct inference that can be reasonably drawn about students' knowledge. Rarely would you want to limit your inference about knowledge to the specific questions asked in a specific format. Generally, you want to make inferences about a broader domain of skills.

Further complicating matters, many people wish to use test scores to draw indirect inferences about why students score the way they do. Indirect inferences can lead to weaker and possibly incorrect interpretations about school programs.

Indirect inferences cannot possibly be accurate unless the direct inference of student achievement is made to the correct domain. Rarely does one wish to limit the inference about knowledge to the specific questions in a test or even the specific objectives tested. For example, if parents want to infer how well their children will do in another school next year, they need to make inferences about the broader domain and not about the specific objectives tested on a particular standardized test. For that inference to be accurate, the instruction must not be limited to the narrow set of objectives of a given test. Thus, for the most typical inferences, the line demarcating legitimate and illegitimate teaching of the test must be drawn between Points 3 and 4.

While it may be inappropriate to prepare students by focusing on the sample of objectives that happen to be tested, you can undertake appropriate activities to prepare students to take standardized tests.

Appropriate Activities to Prepare Students

Ligon and Jones suggest that an appropriate activity for preparing students for standardized testing is *one which contributes to students' performing on the test near their true achievement levels, and one which contributes more to their scores than would an equal amount of regular classroom instruction (1982, p. 1).*

Matter suggests that:

Ideally, test preparation activities should not be additional activities imposed upon teachers. Rather, they should be incorporated into the regular, ongoing instructional activities whenever possible (1986, p. 10) .

If you follow the suggestion by Ligon and Jones, you might spend some time teaching students general test-taking skills that would help them answer questions correctly if they have mastered the objectives. Without some level of test-taking skills, even knowledgeable students could miss an item (or a set of items) because they did not understand the mechanics of taking a test.

Summary

Although the temptation exists to teach too closely to the test, teachers should not be pressured to do so. The inferences you typically wish to draw from test scores are general in nature and will be inaccurate if you limit instruction to the actual objectives sampled in the test or, worse yet, to the actual questions on the test. It is appropriate, however, to spend some instructional time teaching test-taking skills. Such skills are relatively easy to teach and should take up very little instructional time.

IX.

THE DEBATE OVER NATIONAL TESTING

By Carol Boston

Most teachers are comfortable with developing and using tests for classroom purposes, whether to see how much students have learned, to provide a basis for grades, or to gain an understanding of individual students' strengths and weaknesses. As state departments of education move forward with their testing programs, teachers are becoming increasingly familiar with tests used as measures of accountability. A third layer of testing arises on the national level and includes the National Assessment of Educational Progress (NAEP) and President Bush's plan to require states to test third- through eighth-grade students in Title I schools annually in reading and mathematics, with state results verified against NAEP or a commercial test such as the Iowa Test of Basic Skills. This chapter presents various views of the federal role in testing and offers a brief examination of NAEP, "the nation's report card," in both its national sample format and its state administration, which critics fear has the potential to become a *de facto* national test if it is selected as the basis for comparing state tests. Finally, action steps and resources are provided to enable teachers to take part in the ongoing debate about national testing.

Does the United States need to have some kind of test that every student in every state takes to demonstrate mastery of some agreed-upon body of knowledge and skills? Other countries do, but few have a decentralized, diverse education system similar to ours. A national test would require reaching agreement on several issues, including:

- what the test should cover

- what format it should take

- at what point(s) it should be administered

- who should administer it

- whether and how any types of students (e.g., those in special education, those with limited English proficiency) should be exempted or accommodated

- when it should be administered

- how it should be scored

- what the consequences should be for doing well or poorly on it

- how it should fit in with existing state, school district, and classroom standards and assessments

- who should participate in (and pay for) its development

It is important to note here that commercial test publishers have long offered achievement tests (e.g., the Iowa Test of Basic Skills, the California Achievement Test, the Terra Nova) that are administered to schools across the country and normed on national samples but are not in themselves national tests because individual schools, districts, or states decide for themselves whether to use them and which to select. The SAT is probably the most common test administered in the country, but it is intended to measure college-bound students' aptitude for college work, not academic achievement across a wide range of subjects for all students. And it has the ACT as competition.

The question of a true national test is a complicated one, and like many policy matters, it has strong political overtones. Over the past two decades, many policymakers have moved from an initial position of strong support for a national test as an accountability tool to opposition on the grounds that a national test would usher in a national curriculum and lead to further federal involvement in what should be a state and local matter. These policymakers want states to set their own standards without interference from Washington; they see a national test as a somewhat unwelcome effort to dictate what is important for their students to learn.

On the other hand, some policymakers seem to be less troubled by an expanded federal role in testing, but more suspicious about whether national testing would lead to genuine school improvement and higher student achievement or just sort out and penalize low-performing schools and the students in them, who are disproportionately low income and minority. They argue that until there is truly equal opportunity for all students to learn (with equal access to technology, highly qualified teachers, good facilities, and other learning inputs), testing is an empty exercise. Some policymakers also fear that poor test scores might fuel discontent with the public school system and lead to more support for controversial initiatives such as vouchers for private school students.

Those in favor of national tests, on whatever side of the political fence they sit, point to:

- the value of having a common basis for comparing individual, school, district, and state performance

- the importance of specifying content and performance targets to encourage high aspirations and achievement

- the potential motivating effect of tests if results are linked to hiring and college admissions decisions (Davey, 1992)

Those against national tests point to:

- the fallacy that tests alone lead to positive changes in education

- lack of consensus about desired educational outcomes in various subject areas and the pitfalls of attempting to establish a national curriculum

- limitations and biases inherent in testing, particularly multiple-choice tests but also performance-based tests

- short-sightedness in not attempting to address the real equity issues related to the education of minority and low-income students (Davey and Neill, 1992)

As of this writing (Spring 2001), Congress is debating an education bill that requires annual testing of students in grades three through eight in reading and mathematics and includes incentives for high-performing schools and penalties for low-performing ones. This federally mandated testing raises a variety of practical and technical questions, including the following:

- Who will pay the considerable cost of developing and administering additional tests?

- Do states have the technical expertise and personnel to conduct another large-scale assessment and analyze and report results?

- Will the tests be valid and will scores be reliable for high-stakes purposes such as making decisions about which schools receive financial incentives and which are sanctioned for low performance?

- How will existing state tests be linked to each other or to "yardsticks" such as NAEP or commercial tests so that student and school progress can be measured fairly and accurately, particularly if rewards and sanctions are tied to results?

National Assessment of Educational Progress

NAEP is a 32-year-old congressionally mandated project of the National Center for Education Statistics (NCES) within the U.S. Department of Education. The NAEP assessment is administered annually by NCES to a nationally representative sample of public and private school students in grades 4, 8, and 12 to get a picture of what American children know and can do. NAEP results are usually watched closely because the assessment is considered a highly respected, technically sound longitudinal measure of U.S. student achievement.

Two subject areas are typically assessed each year. Reading, mathematics, writing, and science are assessed most frequently, usually at four-year intervals so that trends can be monitored. Civics, U.S. history, geography, and the arts have also been assessed in recent years, and foreign language will be assessed for the first time in 2003. Once exclusively multiple choice, NAEP now includes performance-based items that call for students to work with science kits, use calculators, prepare writing samples, and create art projects.

Students in participating schools are randomly selected to take one portion of the assessment being administered in a given year (usually administered during a one-and-a-half- to two-hour testing period). Achievement is reported at one of three levels: Basic, for partial mastery; Proficient, for solid academic performance; and Advanced, for superior work. A forth level, Below Basic, indicates less-than-acceptable performance. A key feature to keep in mind is that NAEP results are analyzed by groups rather than individual students. The names of participating schools and students are kept confidential; individual scores are not kept or released. In order to gain information about what factors correlate with student achievement, students, teachers and principals at schools participating in NAEP are also asked to complete questionnaires that address such practices as the amount of homework teachers assign and the amount of television students view.

To help states measure students' academic performance over time and to allow for cross-state comparisons, a voluntary state component was added to NAEP in 1990. Now, states can choose to administer NAEP to representative state samples in fourth and eighth grades and receive results reported by subgroup such as student gender, race/ethnicity, and parents' educational level. While participation in the state NAEP and the main NAEP is voluntary, in reality, compliance is quite high. In 2000, for example, 47 states and jurisdictions participated in the state component. This does not replace participation in the main NAEP. The national sample typically involves 100,000 students from 2,000 schools; state samples typically include 2,500 students per subject, per grade, drawn from 100 schools in each participating state (NCES, 1999). As of this writing, legislators are considering expanding the role of state NAEP to serve as a check on results from the proposed states' annual testing of third through eighth graders called for under the Bush education plan. This could mean annual state NAEP testing in reading and mathematics (as opposed to once every four years) for a sample of students in grades four and eight in each state.

A 26-member independent board called the National Assessment Governing Board (NAGB) is responsible for setting NAEP policy, selecting which subject areas will be assessed, and overseeing the content and design of each NAEP assessment. NAGB does not attempt to specify a national curriculum, but rather, outlines what a national assessment should test, based on a national consensus process that involves gathering input from teachers, curriculum experts, policymakers, the business community, and the public. Three contractors currently work directly on NAEP: the Educational Testing Service designs the instruments and conducts data analysis and reporting; Westat performs sampling and data collection activities; and National Computer Systems distributes materials and scores the assessments. The government also contracts for periodic research and validity studies on NAEP.

Tests, Tests Everywhere

While almost every state has implemented some sort of state testing program, the differences in what the tests measure, how they measure it, and how they set achievement levels make it virtually impossible to conduct meaningful state-by-state comparisons of individual student performance. Some people believe state-to-state comparisons are irrelevant because education is a state and local function. Others believe cross-state comparisons will help spur reform and ensure uniformly high-quality education across the country.

Legislation now being debated calls for the use of NAEP or another nationally administered test as a check on the results of annual state tests. Theoretically, a state-level NAEP would yield useful data. In reality, however, NAEP state-level results have sometimes been confusing because achievement levels of students generally appear to be much lower on NAEP than on the state tests. This discrepancy may be attributed to a number of factors, including the following:

- State tests are more likely to be aligned with state curricula than NAEP is.

- State tests and NAEP use different definitions of proficiency.

- State tests and NAEP may use different formats.

- State tests and NAEP differ in terms of who takes them (e.g., whether students in special education or with limited English proficiency are included).

In general, fewer students are judged to reach the Proficient standard on the NAEP reading and math tests than on state tests (GAO, 1998). This discrepancy can lead people who are not aware of the differences in the two types of tests to question the validity of their own state testing programs or the desirability of participating in a federal test program. Using the results of any other nationally normed standardized test poses the same difficulty.

Cost is potentially an additional barrier to nationwide testing of individual students. As part of the debate on voluntary national tests to measure fourth graders' reading proficiency and eighth graders' mathematics proficiency during the Clinton administration, the General Accounting Office (1998) estimated that a per-administration cost of each test would be $12. If the assessments were administered to each of the nation's public and private school children in grades 4 and 8 as was then proposed, the total cost would have been up to $96 million annually, and it was not clear who was going to pay. Most states are already heavily invested in their own state testing programs.

It is difficult to predict how the national testing issue will ultimately be resolved. President Bush's plan calls for expanding testing in most states and gives NAEP and commercial tests a more prominent role than they currently have. Teachers might be torn between continuing to teach the curriculum aligned with their state assessment or switching gears to focus on whatever other test is being used to determine rewards and sanctions. Given the classroom implications of expanded testing, it makes sense for teachers to stay active in the discussion.

Becoming Involved in the National Testing Debate

Follow the progress of the H.R. 1 bill (http://edworkforce.house.gov/), which reauthorizes the Elementary and Secondary Act of 1965 and includes sections related to the annual testing of students in grades 3 through 8.

- Speak out. Teachers offer a valuable front-line perspective on testing. You can let your legislators know your views through a letter or e-mail. Get addresses at http://www.congress.org or call the Capitol switchboard at (202) 224-3121.

- Find out whether your state is involved in the NAEP assessment program. (See http://nces.ed.gov/nationsreportcard, which includes state profiles and a state with summary information and the names of contact people.)

- Visit the NAEP Web site at http://nces.ed.gov/nationsreportcard to see sample questions, answers, frameworks, and classroom exercises in your subject area. How are these items related to your curriculum, instruction, and assessment practices?

PART 2

Essential Concepts

for Classroom Assessment

WRITING MULTIPLE-CHOICE TEST ITEMS

By Jerard Kehoe

This chapter was adapted with from Testing Memo 4: Constructing Multiple-Choice Tests—Part I, Office of Measurement and Research Services, Virginia Polytechnic Institute and State University, Blacksburg, VA 24060.

A notable concern of many teachers is that they frequently have the task of constructing tests but have relatively little training or information to rely on in this task. The objective of this chapter is to set out some conventional wisdom for the construction of multiple-choice tests, one of the most common forms of teacher-constructed tests. The comments that follow are applicable mainly to multiple-choice tests covering fairly broad topic areas.

Before proceeding, it will be useful to establish terms for discussing multiple-choice items. The stem is the introductory question or incomplete statement at the beginning of each item and this is followed by the options. The options consist of the answer—the correct option—and distractors—the incorrect but (we hope) tempting options.

General Objectives

As a rule, one is concerned with writing stems that are clear and concise, answers that are unequivocal and chosen by the students who do best on the test, and distractors that are plausible competitors for the answer as evidenced by the frequency with which they are chosen. Lastly, and probably most important, we should adopt the attitude that items need to be developed over time in the light of evidence that can be obtained from the statistical output typically provided by a measurement-services office (where tests are machine-scored) and from "expert" editorial review.

Planning

The primary objective in planning a test is to outline the actual course content that the test will cover. A convenient way of accomplishing this is to take 10 minutes following each class to list on an index card the important concepts covered in class and in assigned reading for that day. These cards can then be used later as a source of test items. An even more conscientious approach, of course, would be to construct the test items themselves after each class. The advantage of either of these approaches is that the resulting test is likely to be a better representation of course activity than if the test were constructed before or after the course, when we usually have only an optimistic syllabus or a fond memory to draw from. When we are satisfied that we have an accurate description of the content areas, then all that remains is to construct items that represent specific content areas. In developing good multiple-choice items, three tasks need to be considered: writing stems, writing options, and ongoing item development. The first two are discussed in this chapter.

Writing Stems

We will first describe some basic rules for the construction of multiple-choice stems, because they are typically, though not necessarily, written before the options.

1. Before writing the stem, identify the one point to be tested by that item. In general, the stem should not pose more than one problem, although the solution to that problem may require more than one step.

2. Construct the stem to be either an incomplete statement or a direct question, avoiding stereotyped phraseology, as rote responses are usually based on verbal stereotypes. For example, the following stems (with answers in parentheses) illustrate undesirable phraseology:

   What is the biological theory of recapitulation? (Ontogeny repeats phylogeny)

Who was the chief spokesman for the "American System?" (Henry Clay)

Correctly answering these questions is likely to depend less on understanding than on recognizing familiar phraseology.

3. Avoid including nonfunctional words that do not contribute to the basis for choosing among the options. Often an introductory statement is included to enhance the appropriateness or significance of an item but does not affect the meaning of the problem in the item. Generally, such superfluous phrases should be excluded. For example, consider:

    The American flag has three colors. One of them is (1) red (2) green (3) black

    versus

    One of the colors of the American flag is (1) red (2) green (3) black

In particular, irrelevant material should not be used to make the answer less obvious. This tends to place too much importance on reading comprehension as a determiner of the correct option.

4. Include as much information in the stem and as little in the options as possible. For example, if the point of an item is to associate a term with its definition, it would be preferable to present the definition in the stem and several terms as options rather than to present the term in the stem and several definitions as options.

5. Restrict the use of negatives in the stem. Negatives in the stem usually require that the answer be a false statement. Because students are likely to have the habit of searching for true statements, this may introduce an unwanted bias.

6. Avoid irrelevant clues to the correct option. Grammatical construction, for example, may lead students to reject options that are grammatically incorrect as the stem is stat-

ed. Perhaps more common and subtle, though, is the problem of common elements in the stem and in the answer. Consider the following item:

What led to the formation of the States' Rights Party?

    a.   The level of federal taxation

    b.   The demand of states for the right to make their own laws

    c.   The industrialization of the South

    d.   The corruption of federal legislators on the issue of state taxation

One does not need to know U.S. history in order to be attracted to the answer b.

Other rules that we might list are generally commonsensical, including recommendations for independent and important items, and prohibitions against complex, imprecise wording.

Writing Options

Following the construction of the item stem, the somewhat more difficult task of generating options presents itself. The rules we list below are not likely to simplify this task as much as they are intended to guide our creative efforts.

1. Be satisfied with three or four well-constructed options. Generally, the minimal improvement to the item due to that hard-to-come-by fifth option is not worth the effort to construct it. Indeed, all else being the same, a test of 10 items, each with four options, is likely to be a better test than one with nine items of five options each.

2. Construct distractors that are comparable in length, complexity, and grammatical form to the answer, avoiding the use of such words as always, never, and all. Adherence to this rule avoids some of the more common sources of biased

cueing. For example, we sometimes find ourselves increasing the length and specificity of the answer (relative to distractors) in order to insure its truthfulness. This, however, becomes an easy-to-spot clue for the test-wise student. Related to this issue is the question of whether or not test writers should take advantage of these types of cues to construct more tempting distractors. Surely not! The number of students choosing a distractor should depend only on deficits in the content area which the item targets and should not depend on cue biases or reading comprehension differences favoring the distractor.

3.   Options which read "none of the above," "both a. and e. above," "all of the above," etc., should be avoided when students have been instructed to choose the best answer, which implies that the options vary in degree of correctness. On the other hand, "none of the above" is acceptable if the question is factual and this phrase is probably desirable if computation yields the answer. "All of the above" is never desirable, as one recognized distractor eliminates it and two recognized answers identify it.

4.   After the options are written, vary the location of the answer on as random a basis as possible. A convenient method is to flip two (or three) coins at a time with each possible head-tail combination being associated with a particular location for the answer. Furthermore, if the test writer is conscientious enough to randomize the answer locations, students should be informed that the locations are randomized. (Test-wise students know that for some instructors the first option is rarely the answer.)

5.   If possible, have a colleague with expertise in the content area of the exam review the items for possible ambiguities, redundancies, or other structural difficulties. Having completed the items, we are typically so relieved that we may be

tempted to regard the task as completed and each item in its final and permanent form. Yet, another source of item and test improvement is available to us, namely, statistical analyses of student responses.

XI.

MORE MULTIPLE-CHOICE ITEM WRITING DO'S AND DON'TS

By Robert B. Frary

This chapter was adapted from Testing Memo 10: Some Multiple-choice Item Writing Do's And Don'ts, Office of Measurement and Research Services, Virginia Polytechnic Institute and State University, Blacksburg, VA 24060.

The previous chapter gave a few suggestions for item-writing, but only to a limited extent, due to its coverage of other aspects of test development. This chapter extends the list of recommendations for writing multiple-choice items. Some of these recommendations are backed up by psychometric research; i.e., it has been found that, generally, test scores are more accurate indicators of a student's knowledge when these recommendations are followed than when they are ignored. Other recommendations result from logical deduction.

Content

1. **Do** ask questions that require more than knowledge of facts. For example, a question might require  selection of the best answer when all of the options contain elements of correctness. Such questions tend to be more difficult and discriminating than questions that merely ask for a fact. Justifying the "bestness" of the keyed option may be as challenging to the instructor as the item was to the students,

but, after all, isn't challenging students and responding to their challenges a big part of what being a teacher is all about?

2. **Don't** offer superfluous informa-
    tion as an introduction to a ques-
    tion, for example, *"The presence and*

> No superfluous information

association of the male seems to have profound effects on female physiology in domestic animals. Research has shown that in cattle the presence of a bull has the following effect." This approach probably represents an unconscious effort to continue teaching while testing and is not likely to be appreciated by the students, who would prefer direct questions and less to read. The stem just quoted could be condensed to "Research has shown that the presence of a bull has which of the following effects on cows?" (17 words versus 30).

Structure

3. **Don't** ask a question that
    begins, *"Which of the follow-*
    ing is true [or false]?" fol-
    lowed by a collection of

> Stem and options related

unrelated options. Each test question should focus on some specific aspect of the course. Therefore, it's fine to use items that begin, "Which of the following is true [or false] concerning X?" followed by options all pertaining to X. This construction should be used sparingly, however, if there is a tendency to resort to trivial reasons for falseness or an opposite tendency to offer options that are too obviously true. A few true-false questions (in among the multiple-choice questions) may forestall these problems. The options would be: 1) *True* 2) *False.*

4. **Don't** use items like the following:

    What is (are) the capital(s) of Bolivia?
    A. *La Paz* B. *Sucre* C. *Santa Cruz*

1) *A only*   4) *Both A and B*
2) *B only*   5) *All of the above*
3) *C only*

Research on this item type has consistently shown it to be easier and
less discriminating than items with

| Simple structure |

distinct options. In the example above, one only needs to
remember that Bolivia has two capitals to be assured of
answering correctly. This problem can be alleviated by offer-
ing all possible combinations of the three basic options,
namely:

1) *A only*   5) *A and C*
2) *B only*   6) *B and C*
3) *C only*   7) *A, B, and C*
4) *A and B*   8) *None of the above.*

Due to its complexity, however, initial use of this adaptation
should be limited.

Options

5. **Do** ask questions with varying numbers of options. There is
    no psychometric advantage to having a uniform number,
    especially if doing so results in options that are so implausi-
    ble that no one or almost no one marks them. In fact, some
    valid and important questions demand only two or three
    options, e.g., *"If drug X is administered, body temperature will
    probably: 1) increase, 2) stay about the same, 3) decrease."*

6. **Don't** put negative options following a negative stem.
    Empirically (or statistically) such items may appear to per-
    form adequately, but this is probably only because brighter
    students who naturally tend to get higher scores are also bet-
    ter able to cope with the logical complexity of a double neg-
    ative.

7. **Don't** use *"all of the above."* Recognition of one wrong option eliminates "all of the above," and recognition of two right options identifies it as the answer, even if the other options are completely unknown to the student. Some teachers or instructors probably use items with *"all of the above"* as yet another way of extending their teaching into the test (see 2 above). It just seems so good to have the students affirm, say, all of the major causes of a particular phenomenon. With this approach, *"all of the above"* is the answer to almost every item containing it, and the students soon figure this out.

8. **Do** ask questions with *"none of the above"* as the final option, especially if the answer requires computation. Its use makes the question harder and more discriminating, because the uncertain student cannot focus on a set of options that must contain the answer. Of course, *"none of the above"* cannot be used if the question requires selection of the best answer and should not be used following a negative stem. Also, it is important that *"none of the above"* should be the answer to a reasonable proportion of the questions containing it.

9. **Don't** include superfluous information in the options. The reasons given for 8 above apply. In addition, as another manifestation of the desire to teach while testing, the superfluous information is likely to appear on the correct answer: *1) W, 2) X, 3) Y, because ...., 4) Z.* Students are very sensitive to this tendency and take advantage of it.

10. **Don't** use specific determiners in distractors. Sometimes in a desperate effort to produce another, often unneeded, distractor (see 5 above), a statement is made incorrect by the inclusion of words such as *all* or *never*, e.g., *"All humans have 46 chromosomes."* Students who are otherwise ignorant of the topic being tested learn to classify such statements as distractors.

11. **Don't** repeat wording from the stem in the correct option. Again, an ignorant student will take advantage of this practice.

Errors to Avoid

Most violations of the recommendations given thus far should not be classified as outright errors, but instead, perhaps, as lapses of judgment. And, as almost all rules have exceptions, there are probably circumstances where some of 1 to 11 above would not hold. However, there are three not-too-common item-writing/test-preparation errors that represent nothing less than negligence. They are mentioned here to encourage careful preparation and proofreading of tests:

> **OK**
> - Different number of options
> - "None of the above" (sometimes)
>
> **AVOID**
> - Typos
> - Inconsistent grammar
> - Overlapping distractors

Typos are more likely to appear in distractors than in the stem and the correct answer, both of which get more scrutiny from the test preparer. Students easily become aware of this tendency if it is present.

Grammatical inconsistency between stem and options. Almost always, the stem and the correct answer are grammatically consistent, but distractors, often produced as afterthoughts, may not mesh properly with the stem. Again, students quickly learn to take advantage of this foible.

Overlapping distractors, for example: *Due to budget cutbacks, the university library now subscribes to fewer than __?__ periodicals. 1) 25,000; 2) 20,000; 3) 15,000; 4) 10,000*

Perhaps surprisingly, not all students catch on to items like this, but many do. Worse yet, the instructor might indicate option 2 as the correct answer.

Finally, we consider an item-writing foible reported by Smith (1982). What option would you select among the following (stem omitted)?

1) Abraham Lincoln   3) Stephen A. Douglas

2) Robert E. Lee   *4) Andrew Jackson*

The test-wise but ignorant student will select Lincoln because the name represents the intersection of two categories of prominent nineteenth century people, namely, presidents and men associated with the Civil War.

Try this one:

1) before breakfast   3) on a full stomach
2) with meals   4) before going to bed

Three options have to do with eating, and two with the time of day. Only one relates to both. Unfortunately, some item writers consciously or unconsciously construct items of this type with the intersection invariably the correct answer.

XII.

IMPLEMENTING PERFORMANCE ASSESSMENT IN THE CLASSROOM

By Amy C. Brualdi

If you are like most teachers, you probably make it a common practice to devise some sort of test to determine whether a previously taught concept has been learned before introducing something new to your students. Your tests probably contain either completion or multiple-choice items. As you know, it is difficult to write completion or multiple choice tests that go beyond the recall level. For example, the results of an English test may indicate that a student knows each story has a beginning, a middle, and an end. This basic knowledge, however, does not guarantee that the student will write a story with a clear beginning, middle, and end. Because of this, educators have advocated the use of performance-based assessments.

Performance-based assessments "represent a set of strategies for the . . . application of knowledge, skills, and work habits through the performance of tasks that are meaningful and engaging to students" (Hibbard et al., 1996, p. 5). This type of assessment provides teachers with information about how a child understands and applies knowledge. It also enables teachers to integrate performance-based assessments into the instructional process to provide additional learning experiences for students.

Although the benefits of performance-based assessments are well documented, some teachers are hesitant to implement them in their classrooms. Commonly, this is because these teachers feel they don't know enough about how to assess a student's performance fairly (Airasian, 1991). Another reason for reluctance in using performance-based assessments may be previous experiences with them when the execution was unsuccessful or the results were inconclusive (Stiggins, 1994). The purpose of this chapter is to outline the basic steps you can take to plan and execute effective performance-based assessments.

Defining the Purpose of the Performance-Based Assessment

In order to administer any good assessment, you must have a clearly defined purpose. Thus, you must ask yourself several important questions:

- What concept, skill, or knowledge am I trying to assess?

- What should my students know?

- At what level should my students be performing?

- What type of knowledge is being assessed: reasoning, memory, or process (Stiggins, 1994)?

By answering these questions, you can decide what type of activity best suits your assessment needs.

Choosing the Activity

After you define the purpose of the assessment, you can make decisions concerning the activity. There are some things you must take into account before you choose the activity: time constraints, availability of resources in the classroom, and how much data is necessary in order to make an informed decision about the quality of a student's performance. (This consideration is frequently referred to as sampling.)

Ask Yourself

- What am I trying to assess?

- What should the students know?

- What level?

- What type of knowledge?

The literature distinguishes between two types of performance-based assessment activities that you can implement in your classroom: informal and formal (Airasian, 1991; Popham, 1995; Stiggins, 1994). When a student is being informally assessed, he or she does not know that the assessment is taking place. As a teacher, you probably use informal performance assessments all the time. One example of something that you may assess in this manner is how children interact with other children (Stiggins, 1994). You also may use informal assessment to determine a student's typical behavior or work habits.

A student who is being formally assessed knows that you are evaluating him or her. In a formal assessment you may either have the student perform a task or complete a project, and you can either observe his or her performance of specific tasks or evaluate the quality of finished products.

You must keep in mind that not all hands-on activities can be used as performance-based assessments (Wiggins, 1993). Such assessments require individuals to apply their knowledge and skills in context, not merely to complete a task on cue.

Defining the Criteria

After you have determined the activity as well as what tasks will be included in the activity, you need to define which elements of the project or task will enable you to determine the success of the student's performance. Sometimes, you may be able to find these criteria in local and state curriculums or other published documents (Airasian, 1991). Although these resources may prove to be very useful to you, please note that some lists of criteria may include too many skills or concepts or may not fit your needs exactly. With this in mind, you must be certain to review criteria lists before applying any of them to your performance-based assessment.

Most of the time you must develop your own criteria. When you need to do this, Airasian (1991, p. 244) suggests that you complete the following steps:

- Identify the overall performance or task to be assessed, and perform it yourself or imagine yourself performing it.

- List the important aspects of the performance or product.

- Try to limit the number of performance criteria, so they can all be observed during a pupil's performance.

- If possible, have groups of teachers think through the important behaviors included in a task.

- Express the performance criteria in terms of observable pupil behaviors or product characteristics.

- Don't use ambiguous words that cloud the meaning of the performance criteria.

- Arrange the performance criteria in the order in which they are likely to be observed.

You may even wish to allow your students to participate in this process. You can do this by asking them to name the elements of the project or task that they would use to determine how successfully it was completed (Stix, 1997).

Having clearly defined criteria will make it easier for you to remain objective during the assessment. The reason for this is the fact that you will know exactly which skills and/or concepts you are supposed to be assessing. If your class is not already involved in the process of determining the criteria, you will probably want to share them with your students, because being familiar with the criteria will help them know exactly what is expected of them.

Creating Performance Rubrics

As opposed to most traditional forms of testing, performance-based assessments don't have clear-cut right or wrong answers. Rather, there are degrees to which a person is successful or unsuccessful. Thus, you need to evaluate the performance in a way that will allow you to take those varying degrees into consideration. This can be accomplished by creating rubrics.

A rubric is a rating system by which teachers can determine at what level of proficiency a student is able to perform a task or display knowledge of a concept. With rubrics, you can define the different levels of proficiency for each criterion. Like the process of developing criteria, you can either utilize previously developed rubrics or create your own. When using any type of rubrics, you need to be certain that they are fair and simple. Also, the performance at each level must be clearly defined and accurately reflect its corresponding criterion or subcategory (Airasian, 1991; Popham, 1995; Stiggins, 1994).

When deciding how to communicate the varying levels of proficiency, you may wish to use impartial words instead of numerical or letter grades (Stix, 1997). For instance, you may want to use the following scale: *word, sentence, page, chapter, book.* However, words such as *novice, apprentice, proficient,* and *excellent* are frequently used.

As with criteria development, allowing your students to assist in the creation of rubrics may be a good learning experience for them. You can engage students in this process by showing them examples of the same task performed or project completed at different levels and discuss to what degree the different elements of the criteria were displayed. If your students do not help to create the rubrics, however, you will probably want to share those rubrics with your students before they complete the task or project.

Assessing the Performance

Using this information, you can give feedback on a student's performance either in the form of a narrative report or a grade. There are several different ways to record the results of performance-based assessments (Airasian,1991; Stiggins,1994):

- **Checklist Approach**. When using this, a teacher only has to indicate whether or not certain elements are present in the performances.

- **Narrative/Anecdotal Approach**. When teachers use this, they will write narrative reports of what was done during each of the performances. From these reports, teachers can determine how well their students met their standards.

- **Rating Scale Approach**. When teachers use this, they indicate to what degree the standards were met and generally rate criteria on a numerical scale. For instance, a teacher may rate each criterion on a scale of one to five with one meaning "skill barely present" and five meaning "skill extremely well executed."

- **Memory Approach**. When teachers use this, they observe the students performing the tasks without taking any notes. They use the information from their memory to determine whether or not the students were successful. (Please note that this approach is not recommended.)

While it is a standard procedure for teachers to assess students' performance, teachers may wish to allow students to assess their own performances. Permitting students to do this provides them with the opportunity to reflect upon the quality of their work and learn from their successes and failures.

XIII. ◆

SCORING RUBRICS: WHAT, WHEN, AND HOW?

By Barbara M. Moskal

Scoring rubrics have become a common method for evaluating student work in both K-12 and college classrooms. The purpose of this chapter is to describe the different types of scoring rubrics, explain why they are useful, and provide a process for developing them. The chapter concludes with a description of resources that contain examples of the different types of scoring rubrics and further guidance in the development process.

What Is a Scoring Rubric?

Scoring rubrics are descriptive scoring schemes developed by teachers or other evaluators to guide the analysis of the products or processes of students' efforts (Brookhart, 1999). Scoring rubrics are typically employed when a judgment of quality is required and may be used to evaluate a broad range of subjects and activities. One common use of scoring rubrics is to guide the evaluation of writing samples. Judgments concerning the quality of a given writing sample may vary depending upon the criteria established by the individual evaluator. One evaluator may heavily weigh the evaluation process upon the linguistic structure, while another evaluator may be more interested in the persuasiveness of the argument. A high quality essay is likely to have a combination of these and other factors. By developing a pre-defined scheme for the evaluation process, the subjectivity involved in evaluating an essay becomes more objective.

Figure XIII-1 displays a scoring rubric that was developed to guide the evaluation of student writing samples in a college classroom (based loosely on Leydens and Thompson, 1997). This is an example of a holistic scoring rubric with four score levels. Holistic rubrics will be discussed in detail later in this chapter. As the example illustrates, each score category describes the characteristics of a response that would receive the respective score. By having a description of the characteristics of responses within each score category, the likelihood that two independent evaluators would assign the same score to a given response is increased. This concept of examining the extent to which two independent evaluators assign the same score to a given response is referred to as *rater* reliability.

When are Scoring Rubrics an Appropriate Evaluation Technique?

Writing samples are just one example of performances that may be evaluated using scoring rubrics. Scoring rubrics have also been used to evaluate group activities, extended projects, and oral presentations (e.g., Chicago Public Schools, 1999; Danielson, 1997a; 1997b; Schrock, 2000; Moskal, 2000). They are equally appropriate to the English, mathematics, and science classrooms (e.g., Chicago Public Schools, 1999; State of Colorado, 1999; Danielson, 1997a; 1997b; Danielson and Marquez, 1998; Schrock, 2000). Both pre-college and college instructors use scoring rubrics for classroom evaluation purposes (e.g., State of Colorado, 1999; Schrock, 2000; Moskal, 2000; Knecht, Moskal, and Pavelich, 2000). Where and when a scoring rubric is used does not depend on the grade level or subject, but rather on the purpose of the assessment.

Scoring rubrics are one of many alternatives available for evaluating student work. For example, checklists may be used rather than scoring rubrics in the evaluation of writing samples. Checklists are an appropriate choice for evaluation when the information that is sought is limited to the determination of whether specific criteria have been met. Scoring rubrics are based on descriptive scales and support the evaluation of the extent to which criteria have been met.

The assignment of numerical weights to sub-skills within a process is another evaluation technique that may be used to determine the extent to which given criteria have been met. Numerical values, however, do not provide students with an indication as to how to improve their performance. A student who receives a 70 out of 100, may not know how to improve his or her performance on the next assignment. Scoring rubrics respond to this concern by providing descriptions at each level as to what is expected. These descriptions assist students in understanding why they have received a particular score and what they need to do to improve their future performance.

Whether a scoring rubric is an appropriate evaluation technique is dependent upon the purpose of the assessment. Scoring rubrics provide at least two benefits in the evaluation process. First, they support the examination of the extent to which the specified criteria have been reached. Second, they provide feedback to students concerning how to improve their performance. If these benefits are consistent with the purpose of the assessment, then a scoring rubric is likely to be an appropriate evaluation technique.

What Are the Different Types Of Scoring Rubrics?

Several different types of scoring rubrics are available. Which variation of the scoring rubric should be used in a given evaluation is also dependent on the purpose of the evaluation. This section describes the differences between analytic and holistic scoring rubrics and between task specific and general scoring rubrics.

Analytic Versus Holistic

In the initial phases of developing a scoring rubric, the evaluator needs to determine what the evaluation criteria will be. For example, two factors that may be considered in the evaluation of a writing sample are whether appropriate grammar is used and the extent to which the given argument is persuasive. An analytic scoring rubric, much like the checklist, allows for the separate evaluation of each of these factors. Each criterion is scored on a different descriptive scale (Brookhart, 1999).

The rubric that is displayed in Figure XIII-1 could be extended to include a separate set of criteria for the evaluation of the persuasiveness of the argument. This extension would result in an analytic scoring rubric with two factors, *quality of written expression* and *persuasiveness of the argument.* Each factor would receive a separate score. Occasionally, numerical weights are assigned to the evaluation of each criterion. As discussed earlier, the benefit of using a scoring rubric rather than weighted scores is that scoring rubrics provide a description of what is expected at each score level. Students may use this information to improve their future performance.

Occasionally, it is not possible to separate an evaluation into independent factors. When there is an overlap between the criteria set for the evaluation of the different factors, a holistic scoring rubric may be preferable to an analytic scoring rubric. In a holistic scoring rubric, the criteria are considered in combination on a single descriptive scale (Brookhart, 1999). Holistic scoring rubrics support broader judgments concerning the quality of the process or the product.

Electing to use an analytic scoring rubric does not eliminate the possibility of a holistic factor. A holistic judgment may be built into an analytic scoring rubric as one of the score categories. One difficulty with this approach is that an overlap of the criteria set for the holistic judgment and the other evaluated factors cannot be avoided. When one of the purposes of the evaluation is to assign a grade, this overlap should be carefully considered and controlled. The evaluator should determine whether the overlap is resulting in certain criteria being weighted more than was originally intended. In other words, the evaluator needs to be careful that the student is not unintentionally severely penalized for a given mistake.

General Versus Task Specific

Scoring rubrics may be designed for the evaluation of a specific task or of a broader category of tasks. If the purpose of a given course is to develop a student's oral communication skills, a general scoring rubric may be used to evaluate each of the oral presentations given by that student. This approach would allow the student to use the feedback he or she had acquired from the last presentation to improve his or her performance on the next presentation.

If each oral presentation focuses upon a different historical event and the purpose of the assessment is to evaluate the students' knowledge of the given event, a general scoring rubric for evaluating a sequence of presentations may not be adequate. Historical events differ in both influencing factors and outcomes. In order to evaluate the students' factual and conceptual knowledge of these events, it may be necessary to develop separate scoring rubrics

Figure XIII-1
Example of a Scoring Rubric Designed to Evaluate College Writing Samples.

-3-
Meets Expectations for a first Draft of
a Professional Report

- The document can be easily followed. A combination of the following are apparent in the document:

    1. Effective transitions are used throughout.
    2. A professional format is used.
    3. The graphics are descriptive and clearly support the document's purpose.

- The document is clear and concise and appropriate grammar is used throughout.

-2-
Adequate

- The document can be easily followed. A combination of the following are apparent in the document:

    1. Basic transitions are used.
    2. A structured format is used.
    3. Some supporting graphics are provided, but are not clearly explained.

- The document contains minimal distractions that appear in a combination of the following forms:

    1. Flow in thought
    2. Graphical presentations
    3. Grammar/mechanics

Figure XIII-1
(continued)

-1-
Needs Improvement

- Organization of document is difficult to follow due to a combination of the following:

    1. Inadequate transitions
    2. Rambling format
    3. Insufficient or irrelevant information
    4. Ambiguous graphics

- The document contains numerous distractions that appear in a combination of the following forms:

    1. Flow in thought
    2. Graphical presentations
    3. Grammar/mechanics

-0-
Inadequate

- There appears to be no organization of the document's contents.
- Sentences are difficult to read and understand.

for each presentation. A "Task Specific" scoring rubric is designed to evaluate student performances on a single assessment event.

Scoring rubrics may be designed to contain both general and task specific components. If the purpose of a presentation is to evaluate students' oral presentation skills and their knowledge of the historical event that is being discussed, an analytic rubric could be used that contains both a general component and a task specific component. The oral component of the rubric may consist of a general set of criteria developed for the evaluation of oral presentations; the task specific component of the rubric may contain a set of criteria developed with the specific historical event in mind.

How Are Scoring Rubrics Developed?

The first step in developing a scoring rubric is to clearly identify the qualities that need to be displayed in a student's work to demonstrate proficient performance (Brookhart, 1999). The identified qualities will form the top level or levels of scoring criteria for the scoring rubric. The decision can then be made as to whether the information that is desired from the evaluation can best be acquired through the use of an analytic or holistic scoring rubric. If an analytic scoring rubric is created, then each criterion is considered separately as the descriptions of the different score levels are developed. This process results in separate descriptive scoring schemes for each evaluation factor. For holistic scoring rubrics, the collection of criteria is

> Use descriptors rather than judgments.

considered throughout the construction of each level of the scoring rubric and the result is a single descriptive scoring scheme.

After defining the criteria for the top level of performance, the evaluator's attention may be turned to defining the criteria for the lowest level of performance. What type of performance would suggest a very limited understanding of the concepts being assessed? The contrast between the criteria for top-level performance and bottom level performance are likely to suggest appropriate criteria for the middle level of performance. This approach would result in three score levels.

If greater distinctions are desired, then comparisons can be made between the criteria for each existing score level. The contrast between levels is likely to suggest criteria that may be used to create score levels that fall between the existing score levels. This comparison process can be used until the desired number of score levels is reached or until no further distinctions can be made. If meaningful distinctions between the score categories cannot be made, then additional score categories should not be created (Brookhart, 1999). It is better to have a few meaningful score categories than to have many score categories that are difficult or impossible to distinguish.

Each score category should be defined using descriptions of the work rather then judgments about the work (Brookhart, 1999). For example, "Student's mathematical calculations contain no errors," is preferable to, "Student's calculations are good." The phrase "are good" requires the evaluator to make a judgment, whereas the phrase "no errors" is quantifiable. In order to determine whether a rubric provides adequate descriptions, another teacher may be asked to use the scoring rubric to evaluate a sub-set of student responses. Differences between the scores assigned by the original rubric developer and the second scorer will suggest how the rubric may be further clarified.

> **Steps in developing a scoring rubric**
> 1. Identify qualities for the highest score.
> 2. Select analytic or holistic scoring.
> 3. If analytic, develop scoring schemes for each factor.
> 4. Define criteria for lowest level.
> 5. Contrast lowest and highest to develop middle level.
> 6. Contrast other levels for finer distinctions.

Resources

Currently, there is a broad range of resources available to teachers who wish to use scoring rubrics in their classrooms. These resources differ both in the subjects they cover and the level they are designed to assess. The examples provided below are only a small sample of the information that is available.

For K-12 teachers, the State of Colorado (1998) has developed an on-line set of general, holistic scoring rubrics designed for the evaluation of various writing assessments. The Chicago Public Schools (1999) maintain an extensive electronic list of analytic and holistic scoring rubrics that span the broad array of subjects represented throughout K-12 education. For mathematics teachers, Danielson has developed a collection of reference books that contain scoring rubrics appropriate to the elementary, middle, and high school mathematics classrooms (1997a, 1997b; Danielson and Marquez, 1998).

Resources are also available to assist college instructors interested in developing and using scoring rubrics in their classrooms. *Kathy Schrock's Guide for Educators* (2000) contains electronic materials for both the pre-college and the college classroom. In *The Art and Science of Classroom Assessment: The Missing Part of Pedagogy*, Brookhart (1999) provides a brief but comprehensive review of the literature on assessment in the college classroom. This includes a description of scoring rubrics and why their use is increasing in the college classroom. Moskal (1999) has developed a Web site that contains links to a variety of college assessment resources, including scoring rubrics.

The resources described above represent only a fraction of those available. The ERIC Clearinghouse on Assessment and Evaluation (ERIC/AE) maintains a Web site with several additional useful links. One of these, *Scoring Rubrics—Definitions and Constructions* (2000b), specifically addresses frequently asked questions about scoring rubrics. This site also provides electronic links to Web resources and bibliographic references to books and articles that discuss scoring rubrics. For more recent developments within assessment and evaluation, a search can be completed on the abstracts of papers that will soon be available through ERIC/AE (2000a). This site also contains a direct link to ERIC/AE abstracts that are specific to scoring rubrics.

Search engines available on the Web may be used to locate additional electronic resources. When using this approach, the search criteria should be as specific as possible. Generic searches that use the terms "rubrics" or "scoring rubrics" will yield a large volume of references. When seeking information on scoring rubrics from the Web, it is advisable to use an advanced search and specify the grade level, subject area, and topic of interest. If more resources are desired, the search criteria can be expanded.

XIV.

SCORING RUBRIC DEVELOPMENT: VALIDITY AND RELIABILITY

By Barbara M. Moskal and Jon A. Leydens

In the previous chapter, a framework for developing scoring rubrics was presented and the issues of validity and reliability were given cursory attention. Although many teachers have been exposed to the statistical definitions of the terms "validity" and "reliability" in teacher preparation courses, the courses often do not discuss how these concepts are related to classroom practices (Stiggins, 1999). The terms are also addressed in a general way in chapters in the first section of this book. One purpose of this chapter is to provide clear definitions of "validity" and "reliability" and illustrate these definitions through classroom examples. A second purpose is to clarify how these issues may be addressed in the development of scoring rubrics—the descriptive scoring schemes developed by teachers or other evaluators to guide the analysis of the products and/or processes of students' efforts (Brookhart, 1999; Moskal, 2000). The ideas presented here are applicable for anyone using scoring rubrics in the classroom, regardless of the discipline or grade level.

Validity

Validation is the process of accumulating evidence that supports the appropriateness of inferences drawn from student responses for specified assessment uses. *Validity* refers to the degree to which the evidence shows that these interpretations are correct and that the manner in which they are used is appropriate (American Educational Research Association, American Psychological Association and National Council on Measurement in

Education, 1999). Three types of evidence are commonly examined to support the validity of an assessment instrument: content, construct, and criterion. The definitions below of these types of evidence are followed by a discussion of how evidence of validity should be considered in the development of scoring rubrics.

Content-Related Evidence refers to the extent to which a student's responses to a given assessment instrument reflect that student's knowledge of the content area being assessed. For example, a history exam in which the questions use complex sentence structures may unintentionally measure students' reading comprehension skills rather than their knowledge of history. A teacher interpreting a student's incorrect response may conclude that the student does not have the appropriate historical knowledge when actually he or she does not understand the questions. The teacher has misinterpreted the evidence—rendering the interpretation invalid.

Content-related evidence is also concerned with the extent to which the assessment instrument adequately samples the content domain. A mathematics test that primarily includes addition problems would provide inadequate evidence of a student's ability to solve subtraction, multiplication, and division problems. Correctly computing fifty addition problems and two multiplication problems does not provide convincing evidence that a student can subtract, multiply, or divide.

Content-related evidence should also be considered by the person developing scoring rubrics. The task shown in Figure XIV-1, developed by the Quantitative Understanding: Amplifying Student Achievement and Reasoning Project (QUASAR) (Lane, et.al., 1995), requires that the student provide an explanation. The intended content of this task is decimal density. In developing a scoring rubric, a teacher could unintentionally emphasize the nonmathematical components of the task. For example, the resultant scoring criteria may emphasize sentence structure and/or spelling at the expense of the mathematical knowledge the student displays. The student's score, which is interpreted as an indicator of his or her mathematical knowledge, would actually be a reflection of grammatical skills. Based on this scoring system, the resultant score would be an inaccurate measure of the student's mathematical knowledge. This discussion does not suggest that sentence structure and/or spelling cannot be assessed through this task. If the

Figure XIV-1
Decimal Density Task

Dena tried to identify all the numbers between 3.4 and 3.5. Dena said, "3.41, 3.42, 3.43, 3.44, 3.45, 3.46, 3.47, 3.48 and 3.49. That's all the numbers that are between 3.4 and 3.5."

Nakisha disagreed and said that there were more numbers between 3.4 and 3.5.

A. Which girl is correct?

Answer:

B. Why do you think she is correct?

assessment is intended to examine sentence structure, spelling, and mathematics, then the score categories should reflect all of these areas.

Construct-Related Evidence indicates the nature of processes internal to an individual. An example of a construct is an individual's reasoning process. While an individual's reasoning occurs internally, it may be partially displayed through results and explanations. An isolated correct answer, however, does not provide clear and convincing evidence of the nature of the person's underlying reasoning process. Although an answer results from a student's reasoning process, a correct answer may be the outcome of incorrect reasoning. When the purpose of an assessment is to evaluate reasoning, both the product (i.e., the answer) and the process (i.e., the explanation) should be requested and examined.

Consider the problem shown in Figure XIV-1. Part A of this problem requires that the student indicate which girl is correct. Part B requires an explanation. The intention of combining these two questions into a single task is to elicit evidence of the students' reasoning process. If a scoring rubric is used to guide the evaluation of students' responses to this task, that rubric should contain criteria that address both the product and the process. An example of a holistic scoring rubric that examines both the answer and the explanation for this task is shown in Figure XIV-2.

Figure XIV-2
Example Rubric for Decimal Density Task

Proficient: Answer to part A is Nakisha. Explanation clearly indicates that there are more numbers between the two given values.

Partially Proficient: Answer to part A is Nakisha. Explanation indicates that there are a finite number of rational numbers between the two given values.

Not Proficient: Answer to part A is Dena. Explanation indicates that all of the values between the two given values are listed.

NOTE: This rubric is intended as an example and was developed by the authors. It is not the original QUASAR rubric, which employs a five-point scale.

Evaluation criteria within the rubric may also measure factors that are unrelated to the construct of interest. This is similar to the earlier example in which spelling errors were being examined in a mathematics assessment. Here, however, the concern is whether the elements of the responses being evaluated are appropriate indicators of the underlying construct. If the construct being examined is reasoning, then spelling errors in the student's explanation are irrelevant to the purpose of the assessment and should not be included in the evaluation criteria. On the other hand, if the purpose of the assessment is to examine spelling and reasoning, then both should be reflected in the evaluation criteria. Construct-related evidence is that which shows that an assessment instrument is completely and only measuring the intended construct.

In addition to reasoning, other constructs such as problem solving, creativity, writing process, self-esteem, and attitudes may also be examined through classroom assessments. Regardless of the construct, facets that may be displayed and would provide convincing evidence of the students' underlying processes should be first identified and then carefully considered in the development of the assessment instrument and the establishment of scoring criteria.

Criterion-Related Evidence shows the extent to which the results of an assessment correlate with a current or future event. Another way to think of criterion-related evidence is to consider the extent to which a students' performance on a given task may be generalized to other, more relevant activities (Rafilson, 1991).

A common practice in many engineering colleges is to develop courses that "mimic" the working environment of a practicing engineer (e.g., Sheppard, and Jeninson, 1997; King, Parker, Grover, Gosink, and Middleton, 1999). These courses are specifically designed to provide the students with experiences in "real" working environments. Evaluations of these courses, which sometimes include the use of scoring rubrics (Leydens and Thompson, 1997; Knecht, Moskal and Pavelich, 2000), are intended to examine how well prepared the students are to function as professional engineers. The quality of the assessment is dependent upon identifying the components of a student's response to the fabricated environment that will suggest his or her successful performance in the professional environment. When a scoring rubric is used to evaluate performances within these courses, the scoring criteria should address the components of the assessment activity that are directly related to practices in the field. In other words, high scores on the assessment activity should suggest high performance outside the classroom or at the future workplace.

Validity Concerns in Rubric Development

Concerns about the valid interpretation of assessment results should begin before the selection or development of a task or an assessment instrument. A well-designed scoring rubric cannot compensate for a poorly designed assessment instrument. Since establishing validity is dependent on the purpose of the assessment, teachers should clearly state what they hope to learn about the responding students (i.e., the purpose) and how the students will display proficiencies (i.e., the objectives). The teacher should use the stated purpose and objectives to guide the development of the scoring rubric.

In order to ensure that an assessment instrument elicits evidence that is appropriate to the desired purpose, Hanny (2000) has recommended numbering the intended objectives of a given assessment and then writing the number of the appropriate objective next to the question that addresses that objective. In this manner, any objectives that have not been addressed through the assessment will become apparent. This method for examining an assessment instrument may be modified to evaluate the appropriateness of a scoring rubric. First, the purpose and objectives of the assessment should be clearly stated. Next, scoring criteria that address each objective should be developed. If one of the objectives is not represented in the score categories, then the rubric is unlikely to provide the evidence necessary to examine the given objective. If some of the scoring criteria are not related to the objectives, then, once again, the appropriateness of both assessment and rubric is in question. This process for developing a scoring rubric is illustrated in Figure XIV-3.

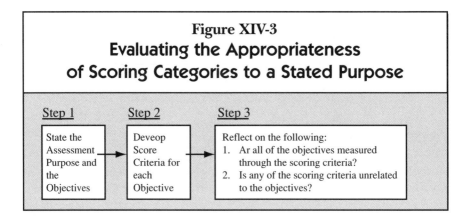

Figure XIV-3
Evaluating the Appropriateness of Scoring Categories to a Stated Purpose

Step 1	Step 2	Step 3
State the Assessment Purpose and the Objectives	Deveop Score Criteria for each Objective	Reflect on the following: 1. Ar all of the objectives measured through the scoring criteria? 2. Is any of the scoring criteria unrelated to the objectives?

Reflecting on the purpose and the objectives of the assessment will also suggest which forms of evidence—content, construct, and/or criterion—should be given consideration. If the intention of an assessment instrument is to elicit evidence of an individual's knowledge within a given content area, such as historical facts, then the appropriateness of the content-related evidence should be considered. If the assessment instrument is designed to measure reasoning, problem solving, or other processes that are internal to the individual and, therefore, require more indirect examination, then the appropriateness of the construct-related evidence should be examined. If the purpose of the assessment instrument is to elicit evidence of how a student will perform outside of school or in a different situation, criterion-related evidence should be considered.

Being aware of the different types of evidence that support validity throughout the rubric development process is likely to increase the appropriateness of the interpretations when the scoring rubric is used. Validity evidence may also be examined after a preliminary rubric has been established. Figure XIV-4 displays a list of questions that may be useful in evaluating the appropriateness of a given scoring rubric with respect to the stated purpose. This table is divided according to the type of evidence being considered.

Many assessments serve multiple purposes. For example, the problem displayed in Figure XIV-1 was designed to measure both students' knowledge of decimal density and the reasoning process they used to solve the problem. When multiple purposes are served by a given assessment, more than one form of evidence may need to be considered.

Another form of validity evidence that is often discussed is consequential evidence. This term refers to examining the consequences or uses of the assessment results. For example, a teacher may find that the application of the scoring rubric to the evaluation of male and female performances on a given task consistently results in lower evaluations for the male students. The interpretation of this result may be that male students are not as proficient as female students within the area being investigated. It is possible that the identified difference is actually the result of a factor unrelated to the purpose of the assessment. In other words, the completion of the task may require knowledge of content or constructs that were not consistent with the original purposes. Consequential evidence refers to examining the outcomes of an assessment and using these outcomes to identify possible alternative interpretations of the assessment results (American Educational Research Association, American Psychological Association, and National Council on Measurement in Education, 1999).

Reliability

Reliability refers to the consistency of assessment scores. For example, on a reliable test, a student would expect to attain the same score regardless of when he or she completed the assessment, when the response was scored, and who scored the response. On an unreliable examination, a student's score may vary based on factors that are not related to the purpose of the assessment.

Figure XIV-4
Questions to Examine Each Type of Validity Evidence

Content	Construct	Criterion
Do the evaluation criteria address any extraneous content?	Are all of the important facets of the intended construct evaluated through the scoring criteria?	How do the scoring criteria reflect competencies that would suggest success on future or related performances?
Do the evaluation criteria of the scoring rubric address all aspects of the intended content?	Are any of the evaluation criteria irrelevant to the construct interest?	What are the important components of the future or related performance that may be evluated through the use of the assessment instrument?
Is there any content addressed in the task that should be evaluated through the rubric, but is not?		How do the scoring criteria measure the important components of the future or related performance?
		Are there any facets of the future or related performances that are not reflected in the scoring criteria?

Many teachers are probably familiar with the terms "test/retest reliability," "equivalent-forms reliability," "split half reliability" and "rational equivalence reliability" (Gay, 1987). Each of these terms refers to statistical methods that are used to establish consistency of student performances within a given test or across more than one test. These types of reliability are of more concern on standardized or high-stakes testing than they are in classroom assessment.

In a classroom, students' knowledge is repeatedly assessed and this allows the teacher to adjust as new insights are acquired.

The two forms of reliability that are typically considered in classroom assessment and in rubric development involve *rater* (or *scorer*) *reliability*. Rater reliability generally refers to the consistency of scores that are assigned by two independent raters and that are assigned by the same rater at different points in time. The former is referred to as *interrater reliability* while the latter is referred to as *intrarater reliability*.

Interrater Reliability refers to the concern that a student's score may vary from rater to rater. Students often criticize exams in which their score appears to be based on the subjective judgment of their instructor. For example, one manner in which to analyze an essay exam is to read through the students' responses and make judgments as to the quality of the students' written products. Without set criteria to guide the rating process, two independent raters may not assign the same score to a given response. Each rater has his or her own evaluation criteria. Scoring rubrics respond to this concern by formalizing the criteria at each score level. The descriptions of the score levels are used to guide the evaluation process. Although scoring rubrics do not completely eliminate variations between raters, a well-designed scoring rubric can reduce the occurrence of these discrepancies.

Intrarater Reliability refers to a situation in which the scoring process of a given rater changes over time. The inconsistencies in the scoring process result from influences that are internal to the rater rather than true differences in student performances. For example, a rater may become fatigued with the scoring process and devote less attention to the analysis over time. Certain responses may receive different scores than they would have had they been scored earlier in the evaluation. A rater's mood on the given day or knowing who a respondent is may also impact the scoring process. A correct response from a failing student may be more critically analyzed than an identical response from a student who is known to perform well. Well-designed scoring rubrics respond to the concern of intrarater reliability by establishing a description of the scoring criteria in advance. Throughout the scoring process, the rater should revisit the established criteria in order to ensure that consistency is maintained.

Reliability Concerns in Rubric Development

Clarifying the scoring rubric is likely to improve both interrater and intrarater reliability. A scoring rubric with well-defined score categories should assist in maintaining consistent scoring regardless of who the rater is or when the rating is completed. The following questions may be used to evaluate the clarity of a given rubric: 1) Are the scoring categories well defined? 2) Are the differences between the score categories clear? 3) Would two independent raters arrive at the same score for a given response based on the scoring rubric? If the answer to any of these questions is "no", then the unclear score categories should be revised.

One method of further clarifying a scoring rubric is through the use of anchor papers. Anchor papers are a set of scored responses that illustrate the nuances of the scoring rubric. A given rater may refer to the anchor papers throughout the scoring process to illuminate the differences between the score levels.

After every effort has been made to clarify the scoring categories, other teachers may be asked to use the rubric and the anchor papers to evaluate a sample set of responses. Any discrepancies between the scores assigned by the teachers will suggest which components of the scoring rubric require further explanation. Any differences in interpretation should be discussed and appropriate adjustments to the scoring rubric should be negotiated. Although this negotiation process can be time consuming, it can also greatly enhance reliability (Yancey, 1999).

Another reliability concern is the appropriateness of the given scoring rubric to the population of responding students. A scoring rubric that consistently measures the performances of one set of students may not consistently measure the performances of another set. For example, if a task is embedded within a context, one population of students may be familiar with that context while another population may be unfamiliar with it. The students who are unfamiliar with the given context may achieve a lower score based on their lack of knowledge of that context. If the same students had completed a different task covering the same material embedded in a familiar context, their scores might have been higher. When the cause of variation in performance and resulting scores is unrelated to the purpose of the assessment, the scores are unreliable.

Sometimes during the scoring process, teachers realize that they hold implicit criteria that are not stated in the scoring rubric. Whenever possible, the scoring rubric should be shared with the students in advance in order to give allow them the opportunity to construct their response in such a way as to provide convincing evidence that they have met the criteria. If the scoring rubric is shared with the students prior to the evaluation, they should not be held accountable for the unstated criteria. Identifying implicit criteria can help the teacher refine the scoring rubric for future assessments.

Conclusions

Establishing reliability is a prerequisite for establishing validity (Gay, 1987). Although a valid assessment is by its nature reliable, the contrary is not true. A reliable assessment is not necessarily valid. A scoring rubric is likely to result in invalid interpretations, for example, when the scoring criteria are focused on an element of the response that is not related to the purpose of the assessment. The score criteria may be so well stated that any given response would receive the same score regardless of who the rater is or when the response is scored.

A final word of caution is necessary concerning the development of scoring rubrics. Scoring rubrics describe general, synthesized criteria that are witnessed across individual performances and, therefore, cannot possibly account for the unique characteristics of every performance (Delandshere and Petrosky, 1998; Haswell and Wyche-Smith, 1994). Teachers who depend solely upon the scoring criteria during the evaluation process may be less likely to recognize inconsistencies that emerge between the observed performances and the resultant score. For example, a reliable scoring rubric may be developed and used to evaluate the performances of preservice teachers while those individuals are providing instruction. The existence of scoring criteria may shift the rater's focus from the *interpretation* of an individual teacher's performance to the mere *recognition* of traits that appear on the rubric (Delandshere and Petrosky, 1998). A preservice teacher who has a unique but effective style may acquire an invalid, low score based on the traits of his or her performance.

The purpose of this chapter was to define the concepts of validity and reliability and to explain how these concepts are related to scoring-rubric development. The reader may have noticed that the different types of scoring rubrics—analytic, holistic, task specific, and general—were not discussed here. (For more on these, see Moskal, 2000.) Neither validity nor reliability is dependent upon the type of rubric. Carefully designed analytic, holistic, task specific, and general scoring rubrics have the potential to produce valid and reliable results.

CLASSROOM QUESTIONS

By Amy C. Brualdi

In 1912, Stevens stated that approximately 80 percent of a teacher's school day was spent asking questions to students. More contemporary research on teacher questioning behaviors and patterns indicates that this has not changed. Teachers today ask between 300-400 questions each day (Leven and Long, 1981).

Teachers ask questions for several reasons (from Morgan and Saxton, 1991):

- The act of asking questions helps teachers keep students actively involved in lessons.

- While answering questions, students have the opportunity to openly express their ideas and thoughts.

- Questioning students enables other students to hear different explanations of the material by their peers.

- Asking questions helps teachers to pace their lessons and moderate student behavior.

- Questioning students helps teachers to evaluate student learning and revise their lessons as necessary.

As one may deduce, questioning is one of the most popular modes of teaching. For thousands of years, teachers have known that it is possible to transfer factual knowledge and conceptual understanding through the process of asking questions. Unfortunately, although the act of questioning has the potential to greatly facilitate the learning process, if done incorrectly, it also has the capacity to turn a child away from learning. The purpose of this chapter is to provide teachers with information on what types of question and questioning behaviors can facilitate the learning process as well as what types of questions are ineffective.

What Is a Good Question?

In order to teach well, it is widely believed that one must be able to question well. Asking good questions fosters interaction between the teacher and his or her students. Rosenshine (1971) found that a large amount of student-teacher interaction promotes student achievement. Thus, one can surmise that good questions foster student understanding. It is important to know, however, that not all questions achieve this.

Teachers spend most of their time asking low-level cognitive questions (Wilen, 1991). These questions concentrate on factual information that can be memorized (for example, In what year did the Civil War begin? or Who wrote *Great Expectations?*). It is widely believed that this type of question can limit students by not helping them acquire a deep, elaborate understanding of the subject matter.

High-level cognitive questions can be defined as questions that require students to use higher order thinking or reasoning skills. By using these skills, students do not only remember factual knowledge. Instead, they use their knowledge to problem solve, to analyze, and to evaluate. It is popularly believed that this type of question reveals the most about whether or not a student has truly grasped a concept because a student needs to have a deep understanding of the topic in order to answer this type of question. Teachers do not use high-level cognitive questions with the same amount of frequency as they ask low-level cognitive questions. Ellis (1993) claims that many teachers rely on low-level cognitive questions in order to avoid a slow-paced lesson, keep the attention of the students, and maintain control of the classroom.

Arends (1994) argues that many of the findings concerning the effects of asking lower-level versus higher-level cognitive questions has been inconclusive. While some studies and popular belief favor asking high-level, other studies reveal the positive effects of asking low-level cognitive questions. Gall (1984), for example, cited that "emphasis on fact questions is more effective for promoting young disadvantaged children's achievement, which primarily involves mastery of basic skills; and emphasis on higher cognitive questions is more effective for students of average and high ability..." (p. 41). Nevertheless, other studies do not reveal any difference in achievement between students whose teachers use mostly high-level questions and those whose teachers ask mainly low-level questions (Arends, 1994; Wilen, 1991). Therefore, although teachers should ask a combination of low-level cognitive and high-level cognitive questions, they must determine the needs of their students in order to know which amount of balance is needed between the two types of questions in order to foster student understanding and achievement.

How to Ask Questions That Foster Student Achievement

In a research review on questioning techniques, Wilen and Clegg (1986) suggest that teachers employ the following research-supported practices to foster higher student achievement:

- phrase questions clearly

- ask questions of primarily an academic nature

- allow three to five seconds of wait time after asking a question before requesting a student's response, particularly when high-level cognitive questions are asked

- encourage students to respond in some way to each question asked

- balance responses from volunteering and nonvolunteering students

- elicit a high percentage of correct responses from students and assist with incorrect responses

- probe students' responses to have them clarify ideas, support a point of view, or extend their thinking

- acknowledge correct responses from students and use praise specifically and discriminately. (p. 23)

What Is A Bad Question?

When children are hesitant to admit that they do not understand a concept, teachers often try to encourage them to ask questions by assuring them that their questions will neither be stupid nor bad. Teachers frequently say that all questions have some merit and can contribute to the collective understanding of the class. The same theory, however, does not apply to teachers. The content of the questions and the manner in which teachers ask them determine whether or not they are effective. Some mistakes that teachers make during the question and answer process include the following: asking vague questions (for example, What did you think of the story we just read?), asking trick questions, and asking questions that may be too abstract for children of their age (for example, asking a kindergarten class the following question: How can it be 1:00 P.M. in Connecticut but 6:00 P.M. in the United Kingdom at the same moment?)

When questions such as those are asked, students will usually not know how to respond and may answer them incorrectly. Thus, their feelings of failure may cause them to be more hesitant to participate in class (Chuska, 1995), evoke some negative attitudes towards learning, and hinder the creation of a supportive classroom environment.

Conclusion

Sanders (1966) stated, "Good questions recognize the wide possibilities of thought and are built around varying forms of thinking. Good questions are directed toward learning and evaluative thinking rather than determining what has been learned in a narrow sense" (p. ix). With this in mind, teachers must be sure that they have a clear purpose for their questions rather than just determining what knowledge a child possesses. Careful planning results in designing questions that can expand student's knowledge and encourage them to think creatively.

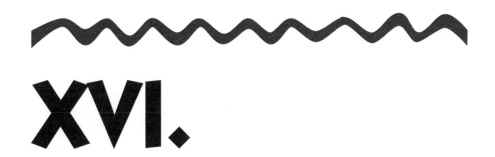

XVI.

TEACHER COMMENTS ON REPORT CARDS

By Amy C. Brualdi

Several times a year, teachers must complete a report card for each student in order to inform parents about the academic performance and social growth of their children. Schools have a variety of ways to document the progress of students. In a majority of schools, teachers usually assign a number or letter grade to the subject or skill areas. In several—mostly elementary—schools, teachers write a descriptive narrative of each child's cognitive and social growth. Other schools have teachers indicate whether a student has acquired various skills by completing a checklist.

Despite the fact that schools have different policies concerning the report card's content and format, most teachers are required to include written comments about a student's progress. Considering the number of students in each classroom, the long span of time needed to complete each report card, and the presence of grades or check marks on the report cards, some may think that comments are nonessential and take up too much of a teacher's time. The purpose of this chapter is to explain why teacher comments on report cards are important, offer suggestions on how to construct effective comments, point out words or phrases to use with caution, and indicate sources of information for report card comments.

Why Are Comments Important?

Grades are designed to define the student's progress and provide information about the skills that he or she has or has not acquired. Nevertheless, grades are often not detailed enough to give parents or the student a thorough understanding of what he or she has actually learned or accomplished

(Wiggins, 1994; Hall, 1990). For example, if a child receives a B in spelling, a report card comment can inform the parent that the child is generally a good speller; however, she consistently forgets to add an es to plural nouns ending with the letters, s and x. Thus, teacher comments often convey whatever information has not been completely explained by the grade.

Well-written comments can give parents and children guidance on how to make improvements in specific academic or social areas. For example, the teacher who wrote the comment above on spelling may wish to say in addition that practice in writing the different plural nouns at home or playing different spelling games may help the child to enhance her spelling skills.

The process of writing comments can also be helpful to teachers because it gives opportunities to be reflective about the academic and social progress of their students. This time of reflection may result in teachers gaining a deeper understanding of each student's strengths and needs.

What Types of Wording Should Teachers Include in Their Comments?

The use of specific comments encourages positive communication between teachers, parents, and students. Written in a positive and informative manner, comments can address a variety of issues while still maintaining the dignity of the child. This is especially important if a child has had difficulty with a particular subject area or controlling his or her behavior over an extended period of time.

Shafer (1997) compiled a list of "effective" comments from a variety of teachers. The boxed lists of words and phrases are just a sampling from her publication, *Writing Effective Report Card Comments* (p. 42-43).

Words And Phrases That Teachers Should Be Cautious About Using

When teachers write comments on report cards, they need to be cognizant of the fact that each child has a different rate of social and academic development. Therefore, comments should not portray a child's ability as fixed and permanent (Shafer, 1997). Such comments do not offer any reason to believe that the child will be successful if he or she attempts to improve.

Also, teachers must be sensitive to the fact that their students will read their comments, and they must be aware that their negative comments may be counterproductive. In addition to the positive comments mentioned above, Shafer (1997) compiled a list of words and phrases that should be avoided or used with caution (p. 45). A sampling is these is included in the adjoining box.

Information Sources To Which Teachers Should Look When Writing Report Card Comments

Teachers should have a plethora of sources from which they can derive information on each child to support the comments that are made on each report card. The most commonly used information is that provided by examples of student work and test results. In addition to these traditional sources, student portfolios as well as formal and informal observations of students offer much useful information. Teachers need to take into account all of these sources in order to provide specific information on the different strengths and weaknesses of each child.

Arter, Spandel, and Culham (1995) define the student portfolio as "a purposeful collection of student work that tells the story of student achievement and growth" (p. 1). A student's portfolio is usually comprised of work that is either the best or most typical example of his or her ability. A portfolio may also contain papers that show the evolution of a particular writing assignment or project. In addition to aiding teachers in keeping track of a student's progress, the portfolio allows the student to chart his or her own academic growth. Because of this, a student should not have many surprises on a report card and will understand how he or she earned particular grades and why different teacher comments were written.

Another rich source of information is the observation of students. Such observations often provide important information that is sometimes difficult to derive from a students' written work. and allow teachers to make comments on students' daily academic and social behaviors. Teacher comments should be written about the students' behaviors in a variety of settings: independent work, cooperative learning groups, and playground or nonacademic interaction (Grace, 1992). Grace also recommends that teachers have the following observations for each child: anecdotal records, a checklist or inventory, rating scales, questions and requests, and results from screening tests.

PART 3

Essential Skills

for Students

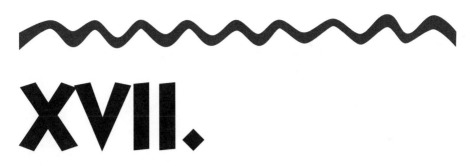

XVII.

IMPROVING THE QUALITY OF STUDENT NOTES

By Bonnie Potts

Much classroom learning at the secondary and postsecondary levels depends on understanding and retaining information from lectures. In most cases, students are expected to take notes and to review them in preparation for testing of lecture material. Such note-taking may serve a two-fold purpose: as a means of encoding the incoming information in a way that is meaningful for the listener, which serves to make the material more memorable from the outset (encoding function); and as a means of simply storing the information until the time of review (external storage function). Although these two purposes often have been treated as though they were mutually exclusive, several studies (e.g., Maqsud, 1980; Knight and McKelvie, 1986) point to a more complex relationship in which the two vary in their relative importance as a function of the individual, the material, and the review and testing conditions.

Do Students Need Help With Their Notes?

Based on several recent investigations, the answer to this question is a resounding "Yes." Of course, some students need more help than others do. Successful students' notes consistently include more of the important propositions, and more propositions overall (though not necessarily more words), than do less successful students' notes (Einstein, Morris, and Smith, 1985). But Kiewra's (1985) summary of the research in this area shows that even successful students generally fail to note many of the important ideas communicated by the lecturer. The best note-takers in these studies (third-year education majors in one study and "A" students in another) included fewer than three-quarters of the critical ideas in their notes. First-year students fared far worse: their notes contained only 11 percent of critical lecture ideas.

How Can Instructors Help?

Given that some of the most important information from lectures is never incorporated into students' notes, some means of helping students prioritize their note-taking certainly is in order. A continuum of approaches exists, from providing full or partial lecture notes to modifying one's lecturing style to facilitate students' own note-taking. None of these is optimal in every case. The type of learning (factual versus analytic or synthetic), the density of the information that must be covered, and the instructor's teaching style all should be considered carefully. The merits and drawbacks of each approach are discussed below.

Providing Full Notes

Kiewra (1985) reported that students who only review detailed notes provided by the instructor after the lecture generally do better on subsequent fact-based tests of the lecture than do students who only review their own notes. In fact, students who did not even attend the lecture but reviewed the instructor's notes scored higher on such tests than did students who attended the lecture and took and reviewed their own notes. This should not be surprising, because unlike the students' notes, the instructor's notes contain all the critical ideas of the lecture.

One might be tempted, however grudgingly, to conclude that providing students with full transcripts of lectures is the best way to optimize their learning of the material. After all, if the goal is to ensure that they don't miss the important ideas, what better way than to hand each student a full text of the lecture? But Kiewra cites evidence that students remember a greater proportion of the information in their own notes than in provided notes, and that students who take the same amount of time to review both their own and the instructor's notes perform best of all on fact-based tests. Interestingly, the pattern of superior performance with provided notes changes when the test involves higher-order learning (e.g., analysis and synthesis of ideas). In such cases, having the instructor's notes does not produce superior performance.

These results suggest that there is some value in having students participate in the note-taking process, however incomplete their notes may be. A
more practical disadvantage to providing full notes is that they may defeat the
purpose of the lecture itself. Even if this is not the case (e.g., if lectures serve
as opportunities for discussion or other interactive forms of learning), the
availability of full notes may encourage absenteeism among students who fail
to recognize the additional benefits of attending lectures. These arguments,
together with many instructors' understandable objections to preparing and
providing full notes, make a compelling case for alternative approaches.

Providing Partial Notes: The Happy Medium

Several independent investigations (see Russell, Caris, Harris, and
Hendricson, 1983; Kiewra, 1985; and Kiewra, DuBois, Christian, and
McShane, 1988) have shown that students are able to achieve the most on
tests when they are provided with only partial notes to review. Specifically, partial notes led to better retention than did comprehensive (full) notes or no
notes, despite the fact that in Russell's study, students expressed an understandable preference for receiving full notes.

Several formats for partial notes have been examined, from outlines, to
matrices, to skeletal guides. Of these, the skeletal format has gained the
widest support (Hartley, 1978; Russell et al., 1983; Kiewra, 1985). In this format, the main ideas of the lecture are provided, usually including the hierar-
chical relationships between them (e.g., by arranging them in outline or
schematic form), and spaces are left for students to fill in pertinent information, such as definitions, elaborations, or other explicative material, as they
listen to the lecture. In Russell's study, students performed especially well
with skeletal notes when the test emphasized practical, rather than factual,
knowledge of the lecture material. They also remained more attentive during
the lecture than did those with other kinds of notes, as evidenced by their
higher scores on test-related items presented during each of the four quarters
of the lecture period.

Hartley (1978) offered three conclusions from naturalistic research with
skeletal notes:

1. Students who get skeletal kinds of notes take about half as
   many notes of their own, compared to students who are not

given notes; yet, students who are given skeletal notes recall more.

2.   The amount of space left for note-taking is a strong influence on the amount of notes that students take (i.e., the more space provided, the more notes taken).

3.   Although skeletal notes lead to better recall than either the student's own notes or the instructor's notes, the best recall occurred when students received skeletal notes before the lecture and the instructor's detailed notes afterward. (Note the similarity between this finding and that in Kiewra's 1985 study.)

Given the opportunities for analysis and synthesis when one has access to both sets of notes in this way, this result is to be expected.

Ideally, then, instructors would be advised to provide both skeletal notes before the lecture and detailed notes afterward in order to afford their students the maximum benefits. But the disadvantages associated with detailed notes have been discussed above, and given these, it seems unlikely that many educators would choose this option. Certainly, there are also those who would disagree in principle with the provision of notes as a remedy for students' difficulties. Instead, it is entirely arguable that emphasis should be placed on helping students improve the quality of their own notes.

How Can Students' Own Notes Be Improved?

Kiewra (1985) offers several suggestions, based on his review of the literature. Some of these call for alterations in the presentation of the lecture. Instructors not only should speak slowly enough to allow students to note important ideas, but also should consider segmenting their lectures. Segmenting involves allowing pauses of three to four minutes for every six or seven minutes of lecture. This enables students to devote their attention to listening during the lecture and then to consolidate the important ideas and paraphrase them during the note-taking pauses. During the lecture phase, students need to be given cues not only to the importance of certain ideas, but also to the kinds of elaboration that they are expected to do on these ideas. In certain kinds of classes (e.g., medical school), where the amount of information that must be presented in a given time is relatively great, it may not be possible to segment the lectures, even though students stand to benefit most from segmenting in such cases. A suggested compromise is to keep information density low whenever possible (limiting the presentation of new ideas to 50 percent of the lecture time), and to provide skeletal notes in increasing quantity as a function of the lecture's increasing information density.

An additional suggestion by Kiewra (1985) is to encourage students to review not only their own notes, but other sources, such as other students' notes and outside texts. Exposure to a variety of renditions of the same material helps to ensure that the material will be preserved in at least one of the presented forms. It also increases the opportunities for more elaborative processing, as the sources are searched and integrated.

Suggestions

- Prepare partial notes for your students.

- Speak slowly so they can write.

- Segment your lectures.

- Highlight important ideas.

- Encourage students to review their notes.

- Encourage students to share notes

XVIII.

HELPING CHILDREN MASTER THE TRICKS AND AVOID THE TRAPS OF STANDARDIZED TESTS

By Lucy Calkins, Kate Montgomery, and Lucy Santman

Adapted with permission from A Teacher's Guide to Standardized Reading Tests. *Knowledge is Power* (1998).

Children can improve and change their test-taking habits if they are taught about their misleading work patterns. Teaching children about the traps they tend to fall into may well be the most powerful specific preparation teachers can give them for the day of the test. By studying the habits of young test takers, we uncovered some of their common mistakes. This chapter lists some of these mistakes and suggests several teaching strategies that may be useful to teachers who are preparing their classes to take standardized tests.

Use the Text to Pick Your Answer

When it comes to choosing an answer, many children are much more likely to turn to their own memories or experiences than to the hard-to-understand text for their answers. This issue becomes even more difficult when the passage is an excerpt from a text with which the students are familiar. Many new reading tests use passages from well-known children's literature, including those stories that have been made into movies. In this case, many students justify their answers by referring to these movies or their memory of hearing the story when they were younger.

While these personal connections are helpful if the student is at a complete loss for an answer, it is essential for children to understand that relying on opinions, memories, or personal experience is not a reliable strategy for finding answers that a test maker has decided are correct. Clearly, many questions asked on the tests require prior knowledge to answer, but the problem comes when students rely exclusively on that prior knowledge and ignore the information presented in the passage. Some things that teachers may wish to do in order to help their students avoid making this mistake include the following:

- Teach students to underline parts of the passage that might be asked in the questions.

- Help children develop scavenger-hunt type lists of things to look for as they read the passages by having them read the questions first.

- Teach students to find out how many questions they can hold in their minds as they read the passage.

- Show children how to fill in all the answers on each test booklet page before filling in the corresponding bubbles on the answer sheet.

- Teach children ways to mark the passage in order to make it easier to go back to find or check specific parts—these include writing key words in the margins and circling or underlining.

- Show students how to use an index card to block out distracting print or to act as a placeholder.

- Retype familiar or easy text to look as daunting and dense as the test passages to give children confidence and experience in the test format..

Sometimes It Is Helpful to Refer to Your Own Life Experiences

In the reading comprehension sections of a reading test, children must find evidence in the passages to support their answers. Yet, there are parts of many reading tests where the only things students can rely on are their own previous experiences. In these sections, students are asked to choose the correct spelling of the underlined word or to choose the word whose meaning is closest to that of the underlined word.

Often students prepare for these sections of the tests by taking practice tests and then going over the answers. It is highly unlikely, however, that any of the same words would appear on the actual test. Therefore, teachers may wish to impress upon children the importance of creating a context for the variety of words that may be found on the test by relating those words to their own personal reading experiences. In order to facilitate that thinking process, teachers may wish to help children ask themselves such questions as, "Have I seen this word before in a book?" "Where have I heard that before?" or "What words or events usually happen around this word?" while they are answering vocabulary or spelling questions.

Learn to Read the Question

It is always assumed that if children have reading troubles, their wrong answers stem from difficulty reading the passages. However, this is not always the case. Sometimes, reading the questions, a much less familiar task, can prove to be the greatest reading challenge for the students. This is because questions such as, "How was the central problem resolved?" or "Which statement is NOT true about the narrator?" are not the types of questions children ask themselves and each other about the books they read.

Studying various types of questions can be a helpful practice for future test takers. Students can become familiar with the types of questions by searching through practice tests and making lists of the question types they find. Although the questions will be different on the day of the test, this exercise may familiarize students with the varieties of questions asked on standardized tests.

Choose the Answer to the Question

Sometimes children choose their answer by finding the first answer choice that matches something in the text. Unfortunately, by not considering what the question was actually asking, they are tricked into choosing the wrong answer simply because it may state a fact that was included in the story.

Working with a partner, a child should figure out what the different questions are asking, and write down his or her paraphrased versions. Many times children will be surprised at how different their paraphrasing is from what the question is actually asking. It may be a good practice for teachers to look at the different paraphrases with the class and discuss which interpretations would help the students and which would lead them astray. This allows students to strengthen their skill of finding the true meaning of the questions.

Risk an Unfamiliar Choice

Frequently, students avoid choosing an answer simply because it contains an unknown word even when they know the other choices are probably wrong. Thus, teachers should advise students not to overlook the possibility that the answer that contains the unfamiliar word may be the correct choice. Teachers often try to teach children a way of narrowing down the answer choices through a process of elimination. Despite the fact that this process can be very helpful, many students eliminate two possibilities and then, from the last two, haphazardly pick one. They don't, it seems, try to figure out a reason to choose one over the other. They seem to assume wrongly that the two choices left are equally possible. However, teachers should teach students that thoughtful elimination of one of the two last possibilities can yield the correct choice.

Check Your Answers

After the harrowing ordeal of taking a standardized test, the last thing students usually want to hear coming from their teacher is, "Did you check your answers?" Frequently, the biggest reason kids hate checking answers is because they have only one strategy for doing so: opening their test booklets to the first passage and beginning again. To them, checking answers means taking the test again. That does not have to be the case, however. There are a variety of different strategies students can use for selectively going back through the test and reconsidering answers. One of these strategies is to check only the problems of which they are unsure. It is unnecessary to return to questions about which they feel fairly confident. They can keep track of the troublesome questions while they are actually taking the test. They can do this in several different ways: jotting down the numbers of the questions on a separate sheet of paper, circling the numbers in the test booklet, etc. They should also know that it is okay to take a short break (stretching in their seats, taking a bathroom or drink break) before going back and checking the answers. This will give them a chance to clear their minds a little bit. Most importantly, students should be taught to attempt to check the answers to the troublesome questions using a new strategy so that they may avoid reusing possibly faulty problem-solving methods.

Setting the Tone for Test Day

Although teachers may do their best to prepare their students for standardized tests, every teacher has stories of children dissolving into tears on the day of tests. Even if their feelings aren't so obvious, all children feel the pressure to do well. Teachers should be sure not to add to the pressure by overreacting to small deeds of misbehavior or by overemphasizing the fact that today is a testing day.

IXX.

ESPECIALLY FOR STUDENTS—MAKING THE A—HOW TO STUDY FOR TESTS

By Diane Loulou

Tests are one method of measuring what you have learned in a course. Doing well on tests and earning good grades begin with good study habits. If your goal is to become a successful student, take the time to develop good study habits.

This chapter offers a plan to help you study for tests. It explains how to prepare for and take tests. Techniques for taking essay, multiple choice, and other types of exams are reviewed. Although these techniques may help you improve your test scores, other factors, such as class participation, independent projects, and term papers also contribute toward grades.

Before the Test

Organization, planning, and time management are skills essential to becoming a successful student; so start studying as soon as classes begin. Read assignments, listen during lectures, and take good classroom notes. Then, reread the assignment, highlighting important information to study. Reviewing regularly allows you to avoid cramming and reduces test anxiety. The biggest benefit is the time it gives you to absorb information.

Read difficult assignments twice. Sometimes a second reading will clarify concepts. If you are having difficulty with a subject, get help immediately. Meet with your teacher or instructor after class, use an alternate text to supplement required reading, or hire a tutor (ask faculty members and other students for referrals).

Review, Review, Review

Plan ahead, scheduling review periods well in advance. Set aside one hour on a Saturday or Sunday to review several subjects. Keep your reviews short and do them often.

- Daily reviews—Conduct short before- and after-class reviews of lecture notes. Begin reviewing after your first day of class.

- Weekly reviews—Dedicate about one hour per subject to review assigned reading and lecture notes.

- Major reviews—Start the week before an exam and study the most difficult subjects when you are the most alert. Study for two to five hours punctuated by sufficient breaks.

Create review tools, such as flashcards, chapter outlines, and summaries. This helps you organize and remember information as well as condense material to a manageable size. Use 3" x 5" cards to review important information. Write ideas, formulas, concepts, and facts on cards to carry with you. Study on the bus, in waiting rooms, or whenever you have a few extra minutes.

Another useful tool is a study checklist. Make a list of everything you need to know for the exam. The list should include a brief description of reading assignments, types of problems to solve, skills to master, major ideas, theories, definitions, and equations. When you begin your final study sessions, cross off items as you review them.

Study Groups

For some subjects, study groups are an effective tool. Study groups allow students to combine resources; members share an academic goal and provide support and encouragement. Such groups meet regularly to study and learn a specific subject.

To form a study group, look for dedicated students—those who ask and answer questions in class, and who take notes. Suggest to two or three that you meet to talk about group goals, meeting times, and other logistics. Effective study groups are limited to five or six people. Test the group first by planning a one-time-only session. If that works, plan another. After several successful sessions, schedule regular meetings.

Set an agenda for each meeting to avoid wasting time. List the material that will be reviewed so members can come prepared. Also, follow a format. For example, begin by comparing notes to make sure you all heard the same thing and recorded important information. Spend 15 to 20 minutes conducting open-ended discussions on specific topics. Then, test each other by asking questions, or take turns explaining concepts. Set aside five to ten minutes to brainstorm possible test questions.

Taking an Exam

On exam day arrive early and get organized. Pay attention to verbal directions as tests are distributed. Read directions slowly. Scan the entire test, noticing how many points each part is worth and estimate the time needed for individual questions. Before you start answering questions, write down memory aids, formulas, equations, facts, and other useful information in the margins.

Check the time and pace yourself. If you get stuck on a question try to remember a related fact. Start from the general and go to the specific. Look for answers in other test questions. Often a term, name, date, or other fact you have forgotten will appear somewhere else in the test. Move on to the next question if memory aids do not help. You can always go back to the question if you have time.

Test-Taking Tips for Different Types of Exams

Multiple Choice—Check the directions to see if the questions call for more than one answer. Answer each question in your head before you look at the possible answers. If you can come up with the answer before you look at the choices, you eliminate the possibility of being confused by them. Mark questions you can't answer immediately and come back to them later.

When taking a multiple-choice exam, guess only if you are not penalized for incorrect answers. Use the following guidelines to make educated guesses:

- If two answers are similar except for one or two words, choose one of these answers.

- If the answer calls for a sentence completion, eliminate the answers that would not form grammatically correct sentences.

- If answers cover a wide range (5, 76, 87, 109, 500) choose a number in the middle.

For machine-graded multiple-choice tests be certain that the answer you mark corresponds to the question you are answering. Check the test booklet against the answer sheet whenever you start a new section and again at the top of each column.

True-false—If any part of a true-false statement is false, the answer is false. Look for key words, i.e., qualifiers like *all, most, sometimes, never* or *rarely*. Questions containing absolute qualifiers such as *always* or *never* often are false.

Open book—When studying for this type of test, write down any formulas you will need on a separate sheet. Place tabs on important pages of the book so that you don't have to waste time looking for tables or other critical information. If you plan to use your notes, number them and make a table of contents. Prepare thoroughly for open-book tests. They are often the most difficult.

Short answer/fill-in-the-blanks—These tests require students to provide definitions or short descriptions (typically a few words or a sentence or two). Study for them, using flashcards with important terms and phrases. Key words and facts will then be familiar and easy to remember as you answer test questions.

Essay—When answering an essay question, first decide precisely what the question is asking. If a question asks you to compare, do not explain. Standard essay question words are listed below. Look up any unfamiliar words in a dictionary.

Before you write your essay, make a quick outline. There are three reasons for doing this. First, your thoughts will be more organized (making it easier for your teacher to read), and you will be less likely to leave out important

Verbs Commonly Used in Essay Questions:		
Analyze	Discuss	Interpret
Compare	Enumerate	List
Contrast	Evaluate	Outline
Criticize	Examine	Prove
Define	Explain	State
Describe	Illustrate	Summarize

facts. Second, you will be able to write faster. Third, if you do not have time to finish your answer, you may earn some points with the outline. Don't forget to leave plenty of space between answers. You can use the extra space to add information if there is time.

When you write, get to the point. Start off by including part of the question in your answer. For example, if the question is, "Discuss the benefits and drawbacks of universal health care coverage to both patients and medical professionals." Your first sentence might read, "Universal health care will benefit patients in the following ways." Expand your answer with supporting ideas and facts. If you have time, review your answers for grammatical errors, clarity, and legibility.

REFERENCES

Chapter I. Testing and Teaching

Rudman, Herbert C. 1989. Integrating testing and teaching. *Practical Assessment, Research and Evaluation*, 1(6). Available online: http://erieae.net/pare/getvn.asp?v=1&n=6

Chapter II. Fundamental Assessment Principles for Teachers and School Administrators

American Educational Research Association, American Psychological Association, and National Council on Measurement in Education. 1999. *Standards for educational and psychological testing.* Washington, D.C.: Authors.

Americal Federation of Teachers, National Council on Measurement in Education, and National Education Association. 1990. *Standards for teacher competence in educational assessment of students.* Washington, D.C.: Authors. Available online: http://www.unl.edu/buros/article3/html

American Psychological Association. 1988. *Code of fair testing practices in education.* Washington, D.C.: Joint Committee on Testing Practices. Available online: http://ericae.net/code.htm

Black, P., and D. Wiliam. 1998. Inside the black box: Raising standards through classroom assessment. *Phi Delta Kappan.* 80(2), 139-148.

Bruner, J. S. 1960. *The process of education.* New York: Vintage Books.

Calfee, R. C., and W. V. Masuda. 1997. Classroom assessment as inquiry. In G. D. Phye (Ed.) *Handbook of classroom assessment: Learning, adjustment, and achievement.* New York: Academic Press.

Cizek, G. J. 1997. Learning, achievement, and assessment: Constructs at a crossroads. In G. D. Phye (Ed.) *Handbook of classroom assessment: Learning, adjustment, and achievement.* New York: Academic Press.

Ebel, R. L. 1962. Measurement and the teacher. *Educational Leadership*, 20, 20-24.

Farr, R., and M. Griffin. 1973. Measurement gaps in teacher education. *Journal of Research and Development in Education*, 7(1), 19-28.

Fleming, M., and B. Chambers. 1983. Teacher-made tests: Windows on the classroom. In W. E. Hathaway (Ed.), *Testing in the schools*. San Francisco: Jossey-Bass.

Gullickson, A. R. 1985. Student evaluation techniques and their relationship to grade and curriculum. *Journal of Educational Research*. 79(2), 96-100.

Gullickson, A. R. 1996. Teacher education and teacher-perceived needs in educational measurement and evaluation. *Journal of Educational Measurement*, 23(4), 347-354.

Impara, J. C., and B. S. Plake. 1996. Professional development in student assessment for educational administrators. *Educational Measurement: Issues and Practice*. 15(2), 14-19.

Mayo, S. T. 1967. *Pre-service preparation of teachers in educational measurement*. Office of Education Bureau of Research. Washington, D.C.: U.S. Department of Health, Education, and Welfare.

McMillan, J. G. 2001. *Essential assessment concepts for teachers and administrators*. Thousand Oaks, California: Corwin Publishing Company.

McMillan, J. H., and S. Nash. 2000. *Teachers' classroom assessment and grading decision making*. Paper presented at the annual meeting of the National Council on Measurement in Education, New Orleans.

National Council on Measurement in Education. 1995. *Code of professional responsibilities in educational measurement*. Washington, D.C.: Author. Available online: http://www.unl.edu/buros/article2.html

Rogosa, D. 1999. *How accurate are the STAR national percentile rank scores for individual students?—An interpretive guide*. Palo Alto, California: Stanford University.

Sanders, J. R., and S. R. Vogel. 1993. The development of standards for teacher competence in educational assessment of students. In S. L. Wise (Ed.) *Teacher training in measurement and assessment skills*. Lincoln, Nebraska: Burros Institute of Mental Measurement.

Schafer, W. D. 1991. Essential assessment skills in professional education of teachers. *Educational Measurement: Issues and Practice*, 10(1), 3-6.

Shepard, L. A. 2000. *The role of assessment in a learning culture.* Paper presented at the annual meeting of the American Educational Research Association. Available online: http://www.aera.net/meeting/am2000/wrap/praddr01.htm

Stiggins, R. J. 2000. *Classroom assessment: A history of neglect, a future of immense potential.* Paper presented at the annual meeting of the American Educational Research Association.

Stiggins, R. J., and N. F. Conklin. 1992. *In teachers' hands: Investigating the practices of classroom assessment.* Albany, New York: State University of New York Press.

Wiggins, G. 1998. *Educative assessment: Designing assessments to inform and improve student performance.* San Francisco: Jossey-Bass.

Chapter III. Traditional and Modern Concepts of Validity

Embretson (Whiteley), S. Construct validity: Construct representation versus nomothetic span. *Psychological Bulletin*, 93, 179-197.

Loevinger, J. 1957. Objective tests as instruments of psychological theory. *Psychological Reports*, 3, 635-694. (Monograph Supplement 9).

Messick, S. 1989. Validity. In R. L. Linn (Ed.) *Educational measurement* (3rd ed.) 13-103. New York: Macmillan.

Messick, S. 1996a. *Standards-based score interpretation: Establishing valid grounds for valid inferences.* Proceedings of the joint conference on standard setting for large scale assessments. Sponsored by National Assessment Governing Board and the National Center for Education Statistics. Washington, D.C.: Government Printing Office.

Messick, S. 1996b. Validity of performance assessment. In G. Philips (Ed.) *Technical issues in large-scale performance assessment.* Washington, D.C.: National Center for Educational Statistics.

Chapter IV. Reliability

Berkowitz, D., B. Wolkowitz, R. Fitch, and R. Kopriva. 2000. *The use of tests as part of high-stakes decision-making for students: A resource guide for educators and policy-makers.* Washington, D.C.: U.S. Department of Education.

Rudner, L. M. 1992. Reducing errors due to the use of judges. *Practical assessment, Research and Evaluation,* 3(3). Available online: http://ericae.net/pare/getvn.asp?v=3&n=3

Chapter V. Norm- and Criterion-Referenced Testing

Anastasi, A. 1988. *Psychological testing.* New York: Macmillan.

Corbett, H. D., and B. L. Wilson. 1991. *Testing, reform and rebellion.* Norwood, New Jersey: Ablex Publishing Company.

Romberg, T. A., L. Wilson, and Khaketla Mamphono. 1991. The alignment of six standardized tests with NCTM standards. In J. K. Stenmark (Ed.) *Mathematics assessment: Myths, models, good questions, and practical suggestions.* Reston, Virginia: National Council of Teachers of Mathematics.

Stiggins, R. J. 1994. *Student-centered classroom assessment.* New York: Merrill.

U.S. Congress, Office of Technology Assessment. 1992. *Testing in America's schools: Asking the right questions.* Washington, D.C.: Government Printing Office. OTA-SET-519.

Chapter VII. Using State Standards and Assessments to Improve Instruction

Black, P. and D. Wiliam. 1998. Inside the black box: Raising standards through classroom assessment. *Phi Delta Kappan,* October. 139-148.

Stiggins, R.J. 1999. Assessment, student confidence, and school success. *Phi Delta Kappan.* November, 191-198.

Chapter VIII. Preparing Students to Take Standardized Achievement Tests

Ligon, G. D., and P. Jones. 1982. Preparing students for standardized testing: One district's perspective. Paper presented at the annual meeting of the American Educational Research Association, New York.

Matter, M. K. 1986. Legitimate ways to prepare students for testing: Being up front to protect your behind. In J. Hall and F. Wolmut (Eds.). *National Association of Test Directors Symposia, 10-11.* Oklahoma City: Oklahoma City Public Schools.

Mehrens, W. A. 1984. National tests and local curriculum: Match or mismatch? *Educational Measurement: Issues and Practice,* 3(3), 9-15.

Metrens, W. A., and J. Kaminski. 1989. Methods for improving standardized test scores: Fruitful, fruitless or fraudulent? *Educational Measurement: Issues and Practices,* 8(1), 14-22.

Shepard, L.A., and A. E. Kreitzer. 1987. The Texas teacher test. *Educational Researcher,* 16(6), 22-31.

Chapter IX. The Debate Over National Testing

Barton, P. E. 1999. Too much testing of the wrong kind; too little of the right kind in K-12 education. A policy information perspective. Princeton, New Jersey: Educational Testing Service. ED 430 052.

Davey, L. 1992. The case for a national test. *Practical Assessment, Research and Evaluation,* 3(1). Available online: http://ericae.net/pare/getvn.asp?v=3&n=1

Davey, L. and M. Neill. 1991. The case against a national test. *Practical Assessment, Research and Evaluation.* 2(10). Available online: http://ericae.net/pare/getvn.asp?v=2&n=10

General Accounting Office. 1998. Student testing: Issues related to voluntary national mathematics and reading tests. Report to the Honorable William F. Goodling, Chairman, Committee on Education and the Workforce, House of Representatives, and the Honorable John Ashcroft, U.S. Senate. Washington, D.C.: Author. ED 423 244.

National Center for Education Statistics. 1999. *The NAEP guide: A description of the content and methods of the 1999 and 2000 assessments.* Washington, D.C.: U.S. Department of Education

Chapter XII. Implementing Performance Assessment in the Classroom

Airasian, P. W. 1991. *Classroom assessment.* New York: McGraw-Hill.

Hibbard, K. M., et al. 1996. A teacher's guide to performance-based learning and assessment. Alexandria, Virginia: Association for Supervision and Curriculum Development.

Popham. W. J. 1995. *Classroom assessment: What teachers need to know.* Boston: Allyn and Bacon.

Stiggins, R. J. 1994. *Student-centered classroom assessment.* New York: Macmillan.

Stix, A. 1997. Empowering students through negotiable contracting., Paper presented at the National Middle School Initiative Conference. Long Island, New York. January 25.

Chapter XIII. Scoring Rubrics: What, When, and How?

Brookhart, S. M. 1999. *The art and science of classroom assessment: The missing part of pedagogy.* ASHE-ERIC Higher Education Report. 27(1). Washington, D.C.: The George Washington University Graduate School of Education and Human Development.

Chicago Public Schools. 1999. Rubric Bank. Available online: http://intranet.cps.k12.il.us/Assessments/Ideas_and_Rubrics/Rubric_Bank/rubric_bank.html

Danielson, C. 1997a. *A collection of performance tasks and rubrics: Middle school mathematics.* Larchmont, New York: Eye on Education Inc.

Danielson, C. 1997b. *A collection of performance tasks and rubrics: Upper elementary school mathematics.* Larchmont, New York: Eye on Education Inc.

Danielson, C., and E. Marquez. 1998. *A collection of performance tasks and rubrics: High school mathematics.* Larchmont, New York: Eye on Education Inc.

ERIC/AE. 2000a. *Search ERIC/AE draft abstracts.* Available online: http://ericae.net/sinprog.htm

ERIC/AE. 2000b. *Scoring rubrics—Definitions and construction.* Available online: http://ericae.net/faqs/rubrics/scoring_rubrics.htm.

Knecht, R., B. Moskal, and M. Pavelich. 2000. The design report rubric: Measuring and tracking growth through success. Paper to be presented at the annual meeting of the American Society for Engineering Education.

Leydens, J., and D. Thompson. 1997. *Writing rubrics design (EPICS) I*, Internal Communication, Design (EPICS) Program, Colorado School of Mines.

Moskal, B. 2000. Assessment resource page. Available online: http://www.mines.edu/Academic/assess/Resource.htm

Schrock, K. 2000. Kathy Schrock's guide for educators. Available online: http://school.discovery.com/schrock-guide/assess.html

State of Colorado. 1998. The rubric. Available online: http://www.cde.state.co.us/cdedepcom/asrubric.htm#writing

Chapter XIV. Scoring Rubric Development: Validity and Reliability

American Educational Research Association, American Psychological Association, and National Council on Measurement in Education. 1999. *Standards for Educational and Psychological Testing.* Washington, D.C.: Authors.

Brookhart, S. M. 1999. *The art and science of classroom assessment: The missing part of pedagogy.* ASHE-ERIC Higher Education Report 27(1). Washington, D. C.: The George Washington University Graduate School of Education and Human Development.

Delandshere. G., and A. Petrosky. Assessment of complex performances: Limitations of key measurement assumptions. *Educational Researcher*, 27(2), 14-25.

Gay, L. R. 1987. Selection of measurement instruments. In Educational Research: *Competetencies for Analysis and Application* (3rd ed.) New York: Macmillan.

Hanny, R. J. 2000. Assessing the SOL in classrooms. Williamsburg, Virginia: College of William and Mary. Available online: http://www.wm.edu/education/SURN/solass.html

Haswell, R., and S. Wyche-Smith. 1994. Adventuring into writing assessment. *College Composition and Communication*, 45, 220-236.

King, R. H., T. E. Parker, T. P. Grover, J. P. Gosink, and N. T. Middleton. 1999. A multidisciplinary engineering laboratory course. *Journal of Engineering Education*, 88(3) 311-316.

Knecht, R., B. Moskal, and M. Pavelich. 2000. *The design report rubric: Measuring and tracking growth through success.* Proceedings of the annual meeting of the American Society for Engineering Education, St. Louis, Missouri

Lane, S., E. A. Silver, R. D. Ankenmann, J. Cai, E. Finseth, M. Liu, M. E. Magone, B. Moskal, C. S. Parke, C. A. Stone, N. Wang, and Y. Zhu. 1995. *QUASAR Cognitive Assessment Instrument (QCAI).* Pittsburgh: University of Pittsburgh, Learning Research and Development Center.

Leydens, J., and D. Thompson. 1997. *Writing rubrics design (EPICS) I,* Internal Communication, Design (EPICS) Program, Colorado School of Mines.

Moskal, B. M. 2000. Scoring rubrics: What, when and how? *Practical Assessment, Research and Evaluation,* 7(3). Available online: http://ericae.net/pare/getvn.asp?v=7&n=3

Rafilson, F. 1991. The case for validity generalization. Practical Assessment, Research and Evaluation, 2(13). Available online: http://ericae.net/pare/getvn.asp?v+2&n=13

Sheppard, S. and R. Jeninson. 1997. Freshman engineering design experiences and organizational framework. *International Journal of Engineering Education,* 13(3), 190-197.

Stiggins, R. J. 1999. Evaluating classroom assessment training in teacher education programs. *Educational Measurement: Issues and Practice,* 18(1), 23-27.

Yancey, K. B. 1999. Looking back as we look forward: Historicizing writing assessment. *College Composition and Communication,* 50, 483-503.

Chapter XV. Classroom Questions

Arends, R. 1994. *Learning to teach.* New York: McGraw-Hill.

Chuska, K. 1995. *Improving classroom questions: A teacher's guide to increasing student motivation, participation, and higher level thinking. Bloomington,* Indiana: Phi Delta Kappa Educational Foundation.

Ellis, K. 1993. Teacher questioning behavior and student learning: What research says to teachers. Paper presented at the 1993 convention of the Western States Communication Association, Albuquerque, New Mexico. ERIC Document Reproduction 359 572.

Gall, M. 1984. Synthesis of research on teachers' questioning. *Educational Leadership*, 42, 40-47.

Leven, T., and R. Long. 1981. *Effective instruction.* Arlington, Virginia.: Association for Supervision and Curriculum Development.

Morgan, N., and J. Saxton. 1991. *Teaching, questioning, and learning,* New York: Routledge.

Rosenshine, B. 1971. *Teaching behaviors and student achievement.* London, England: National Foundation for Educational Research in England and Wales.

Stevens, R. 1912. *The question as a means of efficiency in instruction: A critical study of classroom practice.* New York: Teachers College, Columbia University.

Wilen, W. 1991. *Questioning skills for teachers. What research says to the teacher,* (3rd ed.). Washington, D.C.: National Education Association. (ERIC Document Reproduction 332 983

Wilen, W., and A. Clegg. 1986. Effective questions and questioning: A research review. *Theory and Research in Social Education,* 14(2), 153-161.

Chapter XVI. Teacher Comments on Report Cards

Ater, J. A., V. Spandel, and R. Culham. 1995. Portfolios for assessment and instruction. ERIC Document Reproduction Service ED 388 890.

Grace, C. 1992. The portfolio and its use: Developmentally appropriate assessment of young children. ERIC digest. ERIC Document Reproduction Service ED 351 150.

Hall, K. 1990. Determining the success of narrative report cards. ERIC Document Reproduction Service ED 334 013.

Shafer, S. 1997. Writing Effective Report Card Comments. New York: Scholastic. Amazon.com.

Wiggins, G. 1994. Toward better report cards. Educational Leadership 52(2) 28-37.

Chapter XVII. Improving the Quality of Student Notes

Einstein, G. L., J. Morris, and S. Smith. 1985. Note-taking, individual differences, and memory for lecture information. *Journal of Educational Psychology*, 77, 522-532.

Hartley, J. 1978. Note-taking: A critical review. *Programmed Learning and Educational Technology*, 15, 201-224.

Kiewra, K. A. 1985. Providing the instructor's notes: An effective addition to student notetaking. *Educational Psychologist*, 20, 33-39.

Kiewra, K. A., N. F. DuBois, D. Christian, and A. McShane. 1988. Providing study notes: Comparison of three types of notes for review. *Journal of Educational Psychology*, 80, 595-597.

Knight, L. J., and S. J. McKelvie. 1986. Effects of attendance, note-taking, and review on memory for a lecture: Encoding versus external storage functions of notes. *Canadian Journal of Behavioral Science*, 18, 52-61.

Maqsud, J. 1980. Effects of personal lecture notes and teacher-notes on recall of university students. *British Journal of Educational Psychology*, 50, 289-294.

Russell, I. J., T. N. Caris, G. D. Harris, and W. D. Hendricson. 1983. Effects of three types of lecture notes on medical student achievement. *Journal of Medical Education*, 58, 627-636.

SUGGESTED FURTHER READING

Chapter III. Traditional and Modern Concepts of Validity

American Psychological Association, American Educational Research Association, and National Council on Measurement in Education. 1985. *Standards for educational and psychological testing.* Washington, D.C.: Authors.

Fredericksen, J. R., and A. Collins. 1989. A systems approach to educational testing. *Educational Researcher,* 18(9), 27-32.

Moss, P. A. 1992. Shifting conceptions of validity in educational measurement: Implications for performance assessment. *Review of Educational Research,* 62, 229-258.

Chapter IV. Reliability

Anastasi, A. 1988. *Psychological testing.* New York: Macmillan.

Lyman, H. B. 1993. *Test scores and what they mean.* Boston: Allyn and Bacon.

McMillan, J. H. 2001. *Essential assessment concepts for teachers and administrators.* Thousand Oaks, California: Corwin Publishing Company.

Nunnally, J. C. 1967. *Psychometric theory.* New York: McGraw-Hill. Chapters 6 and 7.

Popham, W. J. 1998. *Classroom assessment, what teachers need to know.* Boston: Allyn and Bacon.

Chapter VI. Some Measurement Concepts

Anastasi. A. 1998. *Psychological testing.* New York: Macmillan.

Lyman, H. B. 1993. *Test scores and what they mean.* Boston: Allyn and Bacon.

McMillan, J. H. 2001. *Essential assessment concepts for teachers and administrators.* Thousand Oaks, California: Corwin Publishing Company.

Chapter VII. Using State Standards and Assessments to Improve Instruction

Neill, D. 1997. Transforming student assessment. *Phi Delta Kappan,* September, 35-36.

Sadler, D. 1989. Formative assessment and the design of instructional systems. *Instructional Science*, 18, 119-144.

Schafer, W., and R. Lissitz. 1987. Measurement training for school personnel: Recommendations and reality. *Journal of Teacher Education*, 38(3), 57-63.

Stiggins, R. J., and N. Conklin. 1992. *In teachers' hands: Investigating the practice of classroom assessment.* Albany: State University of New York Press.

Chapter X. Writing Multiple-Choice Test Items

Airasian, P. 1994. *Classroom assessment,* (2nd ed.) New York: McGraw-Hill.

Cangelosi, J. 1990. *Designing tests for evaluating student achievement.* Boston: Addison-Wesley.

Grunland, N. 1993. *How to make achievement tests and assessments,* (5th ed.). Boston: Allyn and Bacon.

Haladyna, T. M., and S. M. Downing. 1989. Validity of a taxonomy of multiple-choice item-writing rules. *Applied Measurement in Education*, 2(1), 51-78.

Chapter XI. More Multiple-Choice Item Writing Do's and Don'ts

Airasian, P. 1994. *Classroom assessment,* (2nd ed.) New York: McGraw-Hill.

Brown, F. 1983. Principles of educational and psychological testing, (3rd ed.). New York: Holt Rinehart Winston. Chapter 11.

Cangelosi, J. 1990. *Designing test for evaluating student achievement.* New York: Addison-Wesley.

Grunland, N. 1993. *How to make achievement tests and assessments,* (5th ed.). Boston: Allyn and Bacon.

Haladyna, T. M., and S. M. Downing. 1989. Validity of a taxomony of multiple-choice item-writing rules. *Applied Measurement in Education*, 2(1), 51-78.

Kehoe, J. 1995. Writing multiple-choice test items. *Practical Assessment, Research and Evaluation,* 4(4). Available online: http://erocae/met/pare/getvn.asp?v4&n4

Roid, G. H., and T. M. Haladyna. 1980. The emergence of an item writing technology. *Review of Educational Research*, 49, 252-279.

Smith, J. K. 1982. Converging on correct answers: A peculiarity of multiple-choice items. *Journal of Educational Measurement*, 19, 211-220.

Wesman, A. G. 1971. Writing the test item. In R. L. Thorndike (Ed.) *Educational Measurement* (1st ed.), 99-111. Washington, D.C.: American Council on Education.

Chapter XII. Implementing Performance Assessment in the Classroom

Wiggins, G. 1989. A true test: Toward more authentic and equitable assessment. *Phi Delta Kappan*, May, 703-713.

Wiggins, G. 1993. Assessment, authenticity, context, and validity. *Phi Delta Kappan*, November, 200-214.

Wiggins, G. 1998. *Educative assessment: Designing assessments to inform and improve student performance.* San Francisco: Jossey-Bass.

Chapter XV. Classroom Questions

Bloom, B., M. Englehart, E. Furst, and D. Krathwohl (Eds.). 1956. *Taxonomy of educational objectives: The classification of educational goals. Handbook I: Cognitive domain.* New York: David McKay.

Gall. M., 1970. The use of questions in teaching. *Review of Educational Research*, 40, 707-721.

Sanders. N. M., 1966. *Classroom questions: What kinds?* New York: Harper & Row.

Chapter XVII. Improving the Quality of Student Notes

Farr, R. 1991. Portfolios: Assessment in language arts. ERIC digest. ERIC Document Reproduction Service ED 334 603.

Guskey, T. F. 1996. Reporting on student learning: Lessons from the past—Prescriptions for the future. In T. R. Guskey (Ed.). *Association for Supervision and Curriculum Development Yearbook 1996. Communicating Student Progress*, 13-24. Arlington, Virginia: Association for Supervision and Curriculum Development.

Lake, K. and K. Kafka. 1996. Reporting methods in grades K-8. In T. R. Guskey (Ed.). *Association for Supervision and Curriculum Development Yearbook*

1996. *Communicating Student Progress*, 90-118. Arlington, Virginia: Association for Supervision and Curriculum Development.

Peckron, K. B. 1996. Beyond the A: Communicating the learning progress of gifted students. In T. R. Guskey (Ed.). *Association for Supervision and Curriculum Development Yearbook 1996. Communicating Student Progress*, 58-64. Arlington, Virginia: Association for Supervision and Curriculum Development.

Chapter XVIII. Helping Children Master the Tricks and Avoid the Traps of Standardized Tests

Calkins, L., K. Montgomery, and D. Santman. 1998. *A teacher's guide to standardized tests. Knowledge is power.* Portsmouth, New Hampshire: Heinemann.

Mitchell, R. 1992. *Testing for learning: How new approaches to evaluation can improve American schools.* New York: The Free Press.

Perrone, V. (Ed.). 1991. *Expanding student assessment.* Alexandria, Virginia: Association of Supervision and Curriculum Development.

Chapter IXX. Especially for Students—Making the A: How to Study for Tests

Boyd, R. T. C. 1988. Improving your test-taking skills. ERIC digest 101. ERIC Clearinghouse on Tests and Measurement. ED 302-558.

Ellis, D. B. 1985. *Becoming a master student* (5th ed.). Rapid City, South Dakota: College Survival, Inc.

Mercer County Community College. 1992. *Test-taking tips.* Trenton, New Jersey: Author. ED 3511 597.

Withers, G. 1991. *Tackling that test: Everything you wanted to know about taking tests and examinations.* Perth, Australia: Australian Council for Educational Research.